HONDURAS

THE MAKING OF A
BANANA REPUBLIC

ALSO BY ALISON ACKER

Children of the Volcano

HONDURAS

THE MAKING OF A BANANA REPUBLIC

ALISON ACKER

SOUTH END PRESS

The map of Honduras, p. 10, is used with permission of
the Manitoba Council for International Cooperation,
Winnipeg, Manitoba, and the Brandon University
Geography Department, Brandon, Manitoba, Canada.

The map "U.S.-Honduran Military Establishments",
p. 108, is used with permission of the Institute for
Food and Development Policy, (Food First),
San Francisco, U.S.A.

Cover design by Goodness Graphics
Manufactured in Canada

Library of Congress CIP Data

Acker, Alison, 1928-
    Honduras : the making of a banana republic

    Bibliography: p.
    Includes index.

1. Honduras – History.
2. United States – Foreign relations – Honduras.
3. Honduras – Foreign relations – United States.
4. Honduras – Economic conditions.
I. Title.

F1506.A25 1988   972.83 88-11411
ISBN 0-89608-337-3
ISBN 0-89608-336-5 (pbk.)

South End Press,
116 St. Botolph Street,
Boston, MA 02115

95   94   93   92   91   90   89   88
1   2   3   4   5   6   7

To the people of Honduras, who truly deserve our respect and better acquaintance.

Table of Contents

Preface and Acknowledgements

A visit as a journalist to Honduras in 1984 led me to probe more deeply into a perplexing nation that has been ignored too long. Much of the little information that has come to us about Honduras has been filtered through a distinctly North American lens, and my aim is to offset this bias by considering how Hondurans have felt about their own nation, using Spanish sources and interviews with Hondurans as well as the analysis and information provided by the more independent North American historians and commentators.

In the end, much of the credit for any success here is due to the many people who aided my attempts to find out why Honduras has reached its present plight. First, I wish to thank the Hondurans who assisted my research, especially Victor Meza, director of the Centro de Documentación de Honduras, and Dr. Ramón Custodio, president of the Comité en Defensa de los Derechos Humanos de Honduras. The staff of the Honduras Information Center in Boston provided invaluable advice, as did numerous Hondurans who have preferred to remain nameless.

Canadian colleagues who provided assistance include Tim Draimin of the Jesuit Centre for Social Faith and Justice, Liisa North of York University, Jim Handy of the University of Saskatchewan, David and Debra Zakus, Donna and Morris Fine, Louis Torres, Jamie Swift, and the staff of the Canadian Latin American Resource Centre in Toronto. But no book would have emerged from the morass of notes without the patient and perceptive editing of Robert Clarke. Any errors, omissions, or misinterpretations, however, remain my own responsibility.

A.A., Toronto, Ont.

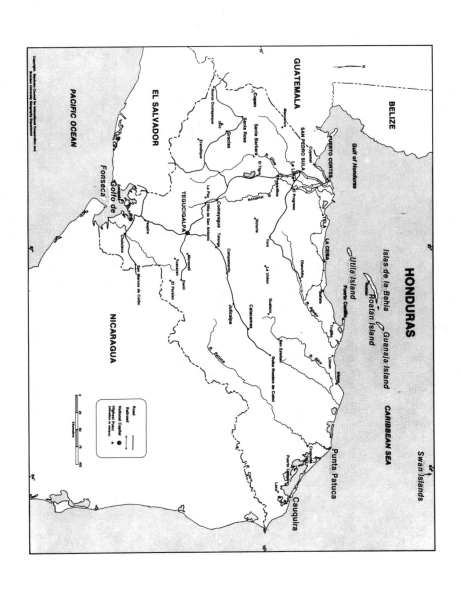

PACIFIC OCEAN

GUATEMALA

EL SALVADOR

Golfo de
Fonseca

BELIZE

Gulf of Honduras

Copan

Nueva Ocotepeque

Santa Barbara

Santa Rosa

Gracias

Erandique

La Paz

Comayagua

Villa de San Antonio

PUERTO CORTES

SAN PEDRO SULA

Cuyamel

Macuelizo

La Lima

El Progreso

El Tigre

TELA

LA CEIBA

Utila Island

Islas de la Bahía

Roatán Island

Guanaja Island

Swan Islands

CARIBBEAN SEA

HONDURAS

Puerto Castilla

Trujillo

Punta Patuca

Cauquira

NICARAGUA

TEGUCIGALPA

Talanga

Yuscaran

Danli

Moroceli

El Paraiso

San Marcos de Colon

Choluteca

Pespire

Victoria

Yoro

La Union

Olanchito

Catacamas

Campamento

Juticalpa

San Esteban

Dulce Nombre de Culmi

Road
Railroad
National Capital
Highest Point
(metres in metres)

Kilometers
0   25   50   75   100

1

An Introduction

"This dump is the centre of the world now."

U.S. GREEN BERET CAPTAIN MICHAEL SHEEHAN,
Honduras, 1981

Honduras should have been a modest, Central American success. It had the right location for trade. It had resources: fifty years ago its bananas were valued as "green gold". Compared to its neighbours, its political system had known a certain degree of democracy and tranquillity, which should have fostered economic and social development. Instead, it became a beggar nation, a sieve for international aid, a country for rent. It sits at the bottom of the Central American list in terms of literacy, health care, nutrition, per capita income, life expectancy, and unemployment.

Blame must be shared by those who have governed Honduras, and by other nations and business enterprises that have taken an interest in Honduras. Together they have created the pattern of dependency characterized by the term "banana republic". Outside aid and investment have not only failed to produce widespread wealth, but have also discouraged domestic responsibility. As a result, Honduras has lost both its own self-respect and the respect of the international community.

Honduras is in the news today only because of U.S. foreign policy in Central America. In recent years we have learned more about the contra fighters and their U.S. advisers than we have about their Honduran hosts. We know as little about Honduran civilian and military leaders as we do about the population as a whole, and all Hondurans tend to get lumped together in a way that would never happen, for instance, with the people and elites of El Salvador or Guatemala.

We know very little about Honduran society and politics. Very few books by Hondurans have been translated into English and relatively few books on

Honduras have been written in English.[1] When Honduras is mentioned in general studies of the region, as historian Thomas P. Anderson notes, the references are usually "reduced to a series of clichés, most of which are inexact and some of which are entirely off the mark".[2]

Often, Honduras is used as a point of comparison with other Central American nations. Its rich are considered not as rich as Guatemala's, its repression not as fierce as El Salvador's, its middle class not as influential as Costa Rica's. It seems that Honduras is often seen merely as a slower version of its neighbouring states, and we have only to wait and see if it turns into another Nicaragua or El Salvador.

Few travellers visit Honduras. Guidebooks disparage it as "neither particularly cheap nor particularly interesting".[3] In the 1980s journalists considered it a three-day country: one day for the U.S. ambassador who really ran the show and two for the contras. A 1986 U.S. magazine article headlined Honduras as "the country of *nada*".[4] Honduras is merely a typical banana republic, a term that has come to mean more than simply a country that exports bananas and is therefore economically dependent on foreign money and markets. It also implies complete political dependency, and, moreover, a country that is "politically unstable, corrupt and backward".[5]

As such, Honduras is not even unique. No wonder, then, that many Westerners tend to lose sight of Honduran identity amid the confusion of Central American states. Outsiders tend to echo the astonishment of Ronald Reagan, who remarked during a Latin American tour in 1982, "You'd be surprised – they're really all different countries".[6]

Honduras is, indeed, a different country, with a unique history and development. No other Central American state has had the same dedication to agrarian reform, the same high level of peasant and union activity. No other Central American state has experienced such stability of traditional liberal and conservative parties. At the same time, no other nation has suffered from such corruption and dependency.

In fact, Honduras has its own identity and its own history, both of which merit wider appreciation. In the ninth century, when Europe was in the so-called dark ages, Copán in western Honduras was the centre of the Mayan civilization's scientific achievements. In 1502 the Honduran shore was the first point on the American continent touched by Christopher Columbus's sailors. Honduras produced one of Central America's most famous Indian rebels, Lempira (his name and profile appear on Honduran currency), as well as the statesman who first unified Central America 150 years ago, Francisco Morazán. Honduras has a history peopled by idealists and rogues, rebels and dictators, dupes and martyrs, conspirators and philosophers. It has been the scene of coups and sieges, betrayals and last stands, fortunes made and fortunes lost.

A country broken by mountains

Honduran geography is as rough as its history, but its location puts it at the region's core. Second largest in area of the Central American nations (following Nicaragua), Honduras is roughly the same size as England or Tennessee. It has both a Caribbean coastline and access to the Pacific; it borders on Guatemala to the west, El Salvador to the southwest, and Nicaragua to the south.

This location might seem to be ideal, giving Honduras convenient access to overseas as well as regional trade. But the Caribbean coast proved treacherous; Columbus searched in vain for a good harbour, and then sailed south. For four centuries, the coast remained an undeveloped line of mosquito-ridden mangrove swamps, while foreign shipping moved to better harbours elsewhere.

Hurricanes have also been a continual danger. In 1974, for example, the Honduran government estimated damage from Hurricane Fifi at $1 million, with ten thousand lives lost.[7] Pirates were another hazard of the Caribbean coast, where proximity to British colonies led to persistent raids and squatter settlements. Pacific ocean access proved to be more of a headache than an asset: the Gulf of Fonseca was shared with Nicaragua and El Salvador on imprecise terms that led to constant dispute.

Instead of offering Honduras a position of power, its location in the midst of squabbling states made it a battle-ground. Deposed presidents and defeated generals often used Honduras as a rallying point before re-entering the fray in their own country.

What seemed like an ideal hemispheric location therefore proved to be full of disappointments. North-south communication and trade were slow to develop and in the end the connecting lines shifted from the Atlantic to the more accessible Pacific coast, where the Pan-American Highway was built during the Second World War. The highway passes only briefly through Honduras and is far away from the capital city, Tegucigalpa, which also remains one of the few world capitals without rail access. Even air access is difficult; landing at Tegucigalpa's Tincontín airport, tucked away into the mountains, gives airline pilots nightmares.

Honduras's mountains are also partly to blame for the lack of economic development. Yet, at first, they seemed to promise infinite mineral wealth. Columbus's sailors picked up shining pebbles on the beach and pocketed them with delight, convinced they were gold washed down from the mountains. They proved to be mere calcite.[8] There was, indeed, gold and silver in the hills, washing down into the coastland area. But once these washings ran out, the gold and silver proved difficult to extract from hard rock that called for the use of expensive machinery. Settlers lured to Honduras by mineral prospects eventually moved south to Peru and Bolivia when the silver boom of South America began.

The mountains, a jumble of razor-backed rock, divide the central plain from the twenty-five-mile-wide Pacific strip and from the Caribbean coast. The eastern regions of Olancho, Colon, and Gracios a Dios, representing over a third of Honduran territory, are also cut off by mountains and remain relatively undeveloped.

The mountainous terrain discouraged native settlement. Even before the Spanish conquest, when Latin America's total native population was about eighty million (compared to only sixty million inhabitants of Europe), barely 800,000 native people lived within what is now Honduras. By 1550 their number had dropped to 132,000 and by 1870 to 47,000, as disease and the harshness of Spanish rule were added to the natural rigours of life.[9]

Later, the harsh terrain discouraged immigration and famine kept down the population of those who did settle and intermingle with the native peoples. While neighbouring countries developed an export agriculture such as cotton or coffee in the nineteenth century, Honduras lacked not only fertile soil and access to markets, but also a pool of labour sufficient for intensive agriculture. Today, with a population of 4.5 million, Honduras has a population density of only 103 per square mile, compared with 603 in El Salvador.[10]

Few of Honduras's mountains are volcanic, so there is little of the fertile laval soil that its neighbours have in abundance. Instead, barely 33 per cent of the land is fit for any sort of agriculture (compared to 64 per cent in El Salvador).[11] Non-arable land is limited to cattle-raising and forestry, and subject to serious erosion because of over-pasturing and indiscriminate logging.

Mountains also impeded the development of a national government. Isolated leaders ruled their own little kingdoms, ignoring or defying centralized authority. Even neighbouring cities were at odds. For three hundred years, Tegucigalpa and Comayagua, barely thirty-one miles apart, disputed their claims to be the nation's capital city, until Tegucigalpa finally asserted its authority in 1880.

Tegucigalpa and San Pedro Sula in the northwest still sometimes operate like capitals of separate states, the first being the traditional seat of government and the second controlling the nation's economic life. Until a modern highway was built in 1970, it took twenty-four hours to cover the 160 miles between them.

The difficulty of building roads impeded development of a marketing structure, which was another reason why Honduras did not share in the coffee boom that created domestic capital and encouraged formation of a local elite in neighbouring nations in the nineteeth century. Isolation also made it impossible for the government in Tegucigalpa to defend the Caribbean coast against pirates, foreign squatters, and, ultimately, the banana companies that were able to run their own empires, virtually separate from their host nation.

Central American Statistics

	Belize	Costa Rica	El Salvador	Guatemala	Honduras	Nicaragua
Life expectancy	66	68	64	60	58	62
Infant mortality per thousand	21	19	53	66	78	43
Literacy	90%	94%	65%	50%	56%	66%
Unemployment & underemployment	14%	20%	45%	65%	70%	25%
Per capita income	$1,140	$1,352	$854	$1,185	$750	$870

Source: *CIA World Fact Book, 1986,* and the *U.N. Statistical Yearbook, 1985*

The reasons for the country's poor record are complex. Any investigation must go beyond Honduran borders to look at outside forces because, sadly, no other nation has been so dominated by foreign interests. Sadly, too, the image of Honduras has already been coloured by those few Westerners who have ventured there. For the most part, they saw it as a colony, through the eyes of the colonizer, applying their own standards and values to what they viewed as a backward "hinterland" – and finding much that was wanting.

2

Through Foreign Eyes

"The people are most uninteresting, chiefly because they are surly to Americans and do not make you feel welcome."

RICHARD HARDING DAVIS, 1896

In Walt Disney comic books there is featured an exotic land called Hondorica, a favourite adventureland of Donald Duck. Hondorica lies east of San Banador, north of Inca Blinca and not far from Brutoland. It is a comic paradise, where shambling peasants welcome Donald and his three cute nephews and gladly hand over all the treasures they have never learned to appreciate. As such, Hondorica represents a synthesis of foreign concepts about Central America, and especially about Honduras.

Hondoricans speak English. They dance and sing a lot. They live in picturesque huts or in ruins. According to Ariel Dorfman, a Chilean sociologist who studied the role of comic book heroes sent out to play in the Third World, they are "affable, ingenuous, happy, trusting children, very easy to placate or deceive".[1]

If Hondoricans represent the "typical good savage" of Jean Jacques Rousseau, Hondorica is a paradise they don't deserve – "a permanent fount of riches and treasures for which they have no use".[2] Hondoricans are children who need to be taught how to operate in a modern world and Donald Duck, it seems, is just the person to teach them.

In his adventures Donald Duck has handed out bars of soap to unwashed Hondoricans. He has saved them from the "mistake" of revolution, accepting bananas and gold bullion in return. He has taught kings how to govern and their subjects how to obey. A child of the North American city, Donald is wiser than the most experienced Hondorican. He also has recourse to adult authority, in the person of Scrooge McDuck, his canny, capitalist uncle. In all of this he has, presumably, delighted millions of readers in the Third World, as well as in North America.

If this caricature of Honduras as Hondorica were an isolated example of North American attitudes, we could perhaps dismiss it as a joke. After all, Instabilidad in Asia and the Unca Uncas of Africa shine even less brightly in the Disney comic sphere. But this is merely one in a series of portrayals that have helped to determine not only how outsiders see Hondurans, but also how the Hondurans see themselves. Given a country that lacks a strong national culture as a defence, a dangerous kind of cultural denigration tends to hold sway. This element of denigration is apparent not just in comic books, but also in novels, travel books, and news reports. Robert W. Desmond refers to this problem in his study of international reporting:

The greatest difficulties in the news relations of Central America with the rest of the world … are two: a tendency on the part of correspondents to sensationalize events and a tendency on the part of some newspaper makers at home to regard that part of the world as slightly comic, or as a field so rich in commercial possibilities as to color the presentation of the news.[3]

Comedy and commercialism have, indeed, distorted our view of Honduras. As a result, Hondurans have become the victims of cultural imperialism in much the same way as those Africans of whom Frantz Fanon wrote:

Every colonized people – in other words, every people in whose soul an inferiority complex has been created by the death and burial of its local cultural originality – finds itself face to face with the language of the civilizing nation, that is, with the culture of the mother country. The colonized is elevated above his jungle status in proportion to his adoption of the mother country's standards.[4]

A colonized nation is highly susceptible to indirect impressions, to outside vision. This is what C. Wright Mills called "living in second-hand worlds", and it is true not only for the colonized. As Mills points out in his book *Power, Politics and People*, we are aware of much more than we have personally experienced and our own experience is always indirect. We receive "meanings" from others, and these meanings determine the quality of our lives. According to Mills:

[People's] experience itself is selected by stereotyped meanings and shaped by ready-made interpretations. Their images of the world, and of themselves, are given to them by crowds of witnesses they have never met and never shall meet….

For most of what he calls solid fact, sound interpretation, suitable presentations, every man is increasingly dependent upon the observation posts, the interpretation centers, the presentation depots which, in contemporary society, are established by means of the cultural apparatus.[5]

For Central America, this "cultural apparatus" often works in the form of the mass media, which has an alarming tendency to create a fictional view of affairs that, consciously or not, is more likely to aid U.S. domestic needs than offer real understanding.[6] Press coverage of Central America tends to be neatly based upon the North American constructs of modernization and security. Because Central America remains "backward" and politically "unstable", only outside interests are capable of producing the type of modernization and security necessary for these nations to be of any use to North American society.

Curiously, North American "interpreters" of Honduras tend to be fascinated by its "primitive" nature while wanting at the same time to exchange it for something more serviceable.

The primitive paradise

The first U.S. representative to tour Honduras, Ephraim George Squier, was lyrical in his praise of the Honduran primitive quality. In 1855 he wrote:

A great variety of trees and abundance of verdure cover the hills and mountains of the northern coast.... Birds of brilliant plumage sparkle in the foliage of the trees, and crowds of monkeys troop among their branches. The tapir, the peccary and the ant-eater live in their shade, and the puma and the cougar lurk in their recesses. Here, too, are found the boa, the bright corral and the deadly tamagas; the vanilla hangs in festoons from the limbs, and the sarsaparilla veins the earth with its healing root. And while silver, imprisoned in flinty quartz or crumbling greenstone, tempts men to labour with the promise of rich reward on the other slope of the continent, here gold glistens in the sands of almost every stream. It is thus that Nature, lavish of her gifts, has comprised within the comparatively narrow limits of Honduras, a variety of scenery, as well as of climate and production, unsurpassed anywhere else on this earth.[7]

Indeed, this same Squier was so enthused about what Honduras had to offer that he adroitly acquired rights to the first railroad company in Honduras. He fought for U.S. control over Honduran ports, and suggested to Honduran politicians that their best future would lie in requesting permission for Honduras to join the United States.

Squier's description led to a romantic tradition of viewing Honduras as a kind of Garden of Eden, with its inhabitants as innocents. So as late as 1971 Franklin Parker, author of *The Central American Republics*, asks, "What is it that makes the people of Honduras attractive?" And responds:

There is a certain primitiveness of character, more discernible here than in most parts of the isthmus, which seems to provide the answer. Persons of this nature are led to accept others as equals and to live non-ostentatiously in their surroundings. The spirit expresses itself in dress which avoids both pomp and prudishness, and in many traits of thought, speech and action. Such a disposition may be accompanied by apathy or even lamentable behaviour stemming from poverty, ill health or ignorance. But one wonders if the Honduras of the future, as she overcomes these problems, must lose her pristine quality. Might she not instead reveal to the world, through the medium of some *aficionado,* the importance of being natural?[8]

The corresponding negative view of "primitive" Hondurans was expressed earlier on, in 1884, by William Wells, who followed Squier as U.S. envoy. Wells concluded: "The major part of the population is careless and indolent, does not value time or take exercise. They do not ride horseback and in consequence are lazy and constitutionally weak."[9]

Wells's comments were echoed by nearly every U.S. visitor to Honduras. Visitors derided the people's ignorance, although many arrived precisely to take advantage of that ignorance. One of them was U.S. explorer J.L. Stephens, who arrived in 1839 and took charge in what was to become typical Yankee fashion. Stephens explains how he acquired as well as explored the Copán ruins:

The reader may be curious to know how old ruins sell in Central America. Like other articles of trade, they are regulated by the quantity of the market and the demand.... I paid fifty dollars for Copán. There never was any difficulty about the price. I offered that sum, for which Don José María thought me only a fool. If I had offered more he would probably have considered me something worse.[10]

The British soon followed Stephens to Copán. Lord Palmerston, British Foreign Secretary in 1854, instructed his chargé d'affaires to the Central American republics to try and get hold of some Copán sculpture for the British Museum. Lord Palmerston also offered a warning:

It appears ... these ruins are held in little or no estimation by the natives of that country.... You will be careful, therefore, that in making inquiries in pursuance of this instruction, that you do not lead the people of the country to attach any imaginary value to things they consider at the present as having no value at all.[11]

Surveyors and mercenaries, salesmen and adventurers gravitated towards "barbarous" Honduras at the end of the nineteenth century as bears to honey. Among them were a number of fugitives from U.S. justice, anxious to enjoy the lack of any extradition treaty between Honduras and the United States.

One such fugitive was the short-story writer O. Henry, who arrived in the

Caribbean port of Trujillo in 1895 to avoid trial on charges of bank forgery. In his short stories he personified Honduras as a half-innocent wanton, comparing Trujillo, for example, to "some vacuous beauty, lounging in a guarded harem".[12]

For O. Henry, Honduras still emanated a whiff of pirate gun-powder. But if the buccaneers had gone, they had left behind a worthy successor, the American salesman:

Gentlemen adventurers throng the waiting rooms of its rulers with proposals for railways and concessions. The little *opera bouffe* nations play at government and intrigue until some day a big, silent gunboat glides into the offing and warns them not to break their toys. And with these changes comes also the small adventurer with empty pockets to fill, light of heart, busy-brained – the modern fairy prince, bearing an alarm clock with which, more surely than by the sentimental kiss, to awaken the beautiful tropics from their centuries' sleep.[13]

American enterprise, it seems, was to be Cinderella's Prince Charming. O. Henry himself left Honduras for the United States, to face his trial and spend time in jail. There he would write the stories that made him famous, romanticizing the "tropics" and mythologizing the small-time U.S. operators. At least he got on well with his Honduran hosts; he turned down invitations from U.S. fellow exiles to take part in some Bonnie and Clyde style banditry, and his six months' stay was memorialized by an elaborate monument to him in the city of Trujillo.

Along with the businessmen came the journalists. Many of them arrived after the war in Cuba ended in 1901, looking for colourful stories. They searched eagerly for news of adventure to brighten up the long drawn-out saga of Panama Canal negotiations, which at the time were the United States' major interest in that part of the world.

One of the most famous journalists was Richard Harding Davis, newspaperman and playwright. He declared Honduras to be "the most exciting country and as despotic as all uncivilized and unstable governments must be".[14] Honduran "surliness" towards Americans aggravated him, but the scenery almost made up for that. He rode the cow-catcher on the front of one of the early banana trains. It was, he wrote, "the most beautiful country I have ever seen and the most barbarous."

It is also the hottest and the most insect-ious and the dirtiest. This latter seems a little view to take of it, but it means a great deal as the insects prevent our doing anything in a natural way, as for instance sitting on the grass or sleeping on the ground or hunting through the bushes.[15]

In another, more reflective, book, Davis voices views that came to typify North American attitudes:

Away from the coasts, where there is fever, Central America is a wonderful country, rich and beautiful and burdened with plenty, but its people make it a nuisance and an affront to other nations.... There is no more interesting question than what is to be done with the world's land which is lying unimproved, whether it shall go to the great power that is willing to turn it to account, or remain with its original owner who fails to understand its value. The Central Americans are like gangs of semi-barbarians in a beautifully furnished house, of which they can understand neither its possibilities of comfort nor its use.[16]

The North American government had been debating how to turn Central America to account ever since the Monroe Doctrine of 1823 established the U.S. right to protect Latin America from any European power. Central America was to be North America's backyard. Later pronouncements elaborated the Monroe Doctrine, claiming the right of the United States to correct Central American "immorality". So, just prior to sending U.S. Marines to Honduras in 1904, President Theodore Roosevelt set down what became known as the Roosevelt Corollary to the Monroe Doctrine:

Chronic wrongdoing or an impotence which results in a general loosening of the ties of civilized society may, in America as elsewhere, require intervention by some civilized nation, and in the Western hemisphere, the adherence of the United States to the Monroe Doctrine may force us, however reluctantly, in flagrant cases of such wrongdoing or impotence, to exercise of an international police power.[17]

To exercise such "moral authority", the United States sent troops to Central America at least ten times between 1900 and 1985. General Smedley D. Butler, who headed some of the early moral rescue missions, was frank about their real motive. He confessed in 1935:

I spent thirty-three years and four months in active service as a member of our country's most agile military force, the Marine Corps. I served in all the commissioned ranks from second lieutenant to major-general. And during that period I spent most of my time being a high-class muscle man for Big Business, for Wall Street and for the bankers. In short I was a racketeer for capitalism.... I helped make Honduras "right" for American fruit companies in 1903.[18]

The U.S. fruit companies protected by Smedley and his Marines also piloted the entrance of Central America into North American popular culture. They provided a new American hero, the tycoon, battling Third World malaria and myopia, crass and immoral perhaps, but nevertheless a hero. One such United Fruit tycoon, Minor Keith, became a character in John Dos Passos's novel *The 42nd Parallel*:

In Europe and the United States, people had started to eat bananas, so they cut down the jungles through Central America to plant bananas and built railroads to haul the bananas and every year more steamboats of the Great White Fleet steamed north loaded with bananas and that is the history of the American empire in the Caribbean and the Panama Canal and the future Nicaraguan canal and the marines and the battleships and the bayonets.[19]

Honduras as hell

Although Dos Passos never visited Central America, the playwright Eugene O'Neill did; his experiences in Honduras were so shattering that they coloured much of his work with a savage misanthropy. Or perhaps he took his own particular hell with him when he went in 1910 to escape the responsibilities of an early and hasty marriage and to try his fortune at panning for gold.

O'Neill quickly caught malaria, had to endure the long mule ride back to Tegucigalpa and recuperated in the U.S. Embassy (now the "old" MacArthur Hotel), where U.S. flags were piled on his bed to stop the chills of fever. He wrote home: "After having been in all the different zones of this country I give it as my fixed belief that God got his inspiration for Hell after creating Honduras.[20]

His recovery did not improve his feelings towards the local people. In a May 15, 1910, letter to his sister, he called them, "the lowest, laziest, most ignorant bunch of brainless bipeds that ever polluted a land."

Until some just fate grows weary of watching the gropings in the dark of these human maggots and then exterminates them, until the Universe shakes these human lice from its sides, Honduras has no future, no hope of being anything but what it is at present – a Siberia of the tropics.[21]

O'Neill continued to carry within him the nightmares he blamed on Honduras. At least they fed an eloquent imagination. No such inspiration can excuse the mindless insults that became a sample of the myriad travel accounts by minor authors, whose attitudes can be surmised by glancing at titles such as *Rotten Republics* or *So Far From God*. This typical sample is from *Tramping through Mexico, Guatemala and Honduras*, published in 1916:

The country is noted chiefly for all the "there is nots". Otherwise one has the impression of watching peculiarly stultified children playing at being a republic. The nation is a large farm in area and a poorly run farm in addition.... One woman at first boldly refused to allow her picture to be taken, but, so weak-willed are the people of Honduras that a white man can, with patience, in no time force them to do his bidding by sheer force of will by merely looking long and forcibly at them.[22]

The author, Harry Franck, considered the "Honduran wild men" to be "less human" than those he had met in Malaya.

In 1934, Aldous Huxley was disappointed by the non-Indian Honduran peasants when he arrived in Copán by air after a stay in the more ethnically interesting Guatemala:

We came back from the ruins to find the entire population of Copán clustered round our aeroplane, like a crowd of Breughel's peasants round a crucifixion. Some were standing: some, with the air of people who had come out for a long day's pleasure, were sitting in the shade of our wings and picnicking. They were a villainous set of men and women; not Indian, but low *ladino*, squalid and dirty as only the poverty-stricken half-caste, with a touch of white blood and a sense of superiority to all the traditional decencies of the inferior race, can be dirty and squalid.[23]

In the 1980s, novelist and travel writer Paul Theroux didn't find much to respect in Honduras either. His novel, *The Mosquito Coast,* set in the Honduran Mosquitia, is a nightmare as horrific as the Congo of Joseph Conrad's *Heart of Darkness.* His hero, a U.S. inventor and self-made man attempting to start a better life away from U.S. decadence, arrives at La Ceiba on the Honduran Caribbean coast:

"I can't see anyone invading this town. Can you, mother?"
"Why would they bother?"
"That's what I mean."[24]

Later the narrator sums up his first days in La Ceiba:

That was Honduras, so far. Dead dogs and vultures, a dirty beach and chicken huts and roads leading nowhere. The view from the ship had been like a picture but now we were inside that picture. It was all hunger and noise and cruelty.[25]

Theroux, like O'Neill, presents Honduras as a dangerous, irrational universe. But his hero proves to be more manic than the chattering "savages" he seeks to lead towards enlightenment. In much the same way, the North American popular culture that has accrued around the image of the banana republic contains an element of irrationality that may say more about North Americans than Central Americans.

23

Bananaland

In a zany study of the banana, a book bound in banana yellow and titled *The Total Banana*, Alex Abella describes, without a trace of mockery, the "banana madness" that swept through the United States in the early twentieth century. American free enterprise, he suggests, made the banana more than a fruit; it made it "fun". He explains:

In 1920, the themes of low comedy and politics (which cynics might say are identical) were wedded to the banana ... the waggish spirit of the banana was reborn in the figure of Carmen Miranda, who reached her banana apotheosis in the film *The Gang's All Here* in which a line of chorines paid homage to her, waving giant papier-mache bananas in her direction.[26]

The banana, says Abella, is "an image of the tropics, where everything is in perpetual slow motion, where no one needs or desires work, where there is food for the hungry". The folk of such a place could not be expected to profit from their own resources. It was "the Yankee traders [who] found it, grew it and sold it all over the world, transforming the tropical hybrid with a two-week life span into the most common fruit on earth".[27]

The banana companies got rich, while the banana republics merely earned a few laughs, the sort of laughs that accompanied vaudeville pratfalls on a banana skin, or snickers about the banana's phallic shape. Honduras itself gets barely a mention in Abella's book. Probably it would best fit into his glossary of banana terms, where "third banana" is defined as "a stage comic who takes a fall" – as Honduras has surely been doing for years.[28] The mid-century U.S. attitude is typified by the huge 1961 *Life Pictorial Atlas of the World*, which carelessly explains away the country in one sentence: "A great banana exporter, Honduras has 1,000 miles of railroad, 900 of which belong to U.S. fruit companies."[29]

It seems as if every writer turns comic when trying to convey the realities of Honduras. William Krehm, covering Central America in the 1940s for *Time* magazine, was eventually fired because his reports conflicted with State Department views. But even Krehm slipped into comic pathos when describing his visit to Honduras in 1944:

Of all the Central American republics, Honduras was the most woebegone. With no other communication to the outside world than planes and mud-tracks, Tegucigalpa breathed a spiritual desolation that one found in none of the other capitals.... Somehow history cheated Honduras and left it a moldy nook, whose yokel setting made its very tragedy just a mite ludicrous. Even the statue of Morazán in Tegucigalpa's central square, where the band plays every Sunday night, is not really Morazán, as the inscription states, but – of all things – Marshal Ney. A commission was sent to Europe in the last century to order a statue of Morazán, but ran out of funds; they were thus reduced to buying up, cheap, an equestrian figure of the Marshal.

That is the sort of thing that happens to all that Honduras sets its heart on.[30]

Unable to strike back, Hondurans have turned bitter. An 1984 editorial in *El Tiempo,* the closest Honduras comes to a progressive daily newspaper, expresses Honduran resentment: "Every time the name of our country appears with great prodigality in the international press, it means that something bad has happened. Never, or hardly ever, are we mentioned for some good action, for something we could really feel proud of."[31]

Honduran politicians, for their part, regularly call for campaigns to rescue the nation's dignity, but have so far failed to ignite much of a spark in a population that often seems resigned to frustration and despair. Honduran history has shown so much failure that it is hard for them to believe in any other possibilities.

3

The Spanish Empire

"I don't know what will happen to this land, but it seems under the influence of a planet that will not let it sleep."

FRANCISCO DE MONTEJO, Governor of Honduras, 1537

Remarkably little is known about the first Hondurans who, like all indigenous Americans, were part of a chain of people coming from Asia. There were, apparently, hunting and gathering tribes in the Department of Intibuca, in western Honduras, six thousand years before Christ. Artifacts reveal very early agricultural people who used spears armed with quartz or obsidian tips. By 1500 BC, tribes were living in huts roofed with palm leaves, not much different from the housing of thousands of Honduran peasants today. They used stone mills to grind corn, made solid clay figures, and kept bees. Archeologists found a skeleton of a child adorned with a necklace of white shells and a jade pendant, and with a belt made up of more than ninety jade beads. In fact, long before the beginning of the Mayan civilization, the Indians of Honduras had developed a complex society with considerable class divisions, hereditary government, and a military organization.[1]

However, none of these accomplishments compares with those of the Mayan civilization, which lasted from 250 to 850 AD. Copán, in western Honduras, was established around 450 AD but when Columbus reached Honduran shores in 1502, it was an overgrown ruin, abandoned some seven hundred years before. At the height of Mayan power Copán was part of an empire of three million people, whose civilization in many ways surpassed any other in the known world at that time.

The great Mayan cities were more like independent city states than part of a larger political structure. They supported substantial permanent populations and depended upon intensive agricultural techniques. Priests and intellectuals formed the hierarchy of power, and it was at Copán that most of the Mayan scientific developments took place. The Mayans reached a mastery of astronomy that enabled them to predict solar eclipses and measure the revolutions of the planet Venus with utmost accuracy. They invented a calendar so nearly perfect that its error in computation was less than twenty-four hours in a thousand years. They invented a numerical system using the concept of zero. They built temples 115 feet high; they invented the corbelled arch, and laid out a ceremonial court that could seat fifty thousand people. Throughout the plazas they erected thirty-eight stellae, carved monuments to commemorate Mayan leaders. They carved storm gods and turtles, singing girls and serpent birds, sky monsters, and the bat god of twilight.

Columbus's sailors probably met some of the descendants of the Mayans when a seventy-foot canoe "which had a roof of palm leaves not very different from the style of gondolas in Venice" paddled up to the Spanish anchorage at Guanaja, off the Honduran coast, on July 30, 1502. Honduran historian Longino Becerra quotes Bartolomé, the brother of Christopher Columbus:

Under the roof were the children, the women and all their belongings and wares. The men, about 25 of them, had no desire to defend themselves, so we took the canoe without a struggle and had it taken to our ships, where the Admiral gave thanks to God, seeing that a sample of the things of that land had been furnished without trouble or danger.[2]

These Indians were probably traders, Mayan descendants, travelling from the Yucatan Peninsula. The local people encountered by the Spaniards were hunters and gatherers, probably Payas or Jicaques, whose ancestors had once been part of the Mayan empire but who did not share the same level of Mayan civilization. Fernando, the son of Christopher Columbus, also reported that the local people drank maize wine "similar to the beer in England" and used cocoa beans for money, "for when they were taken into the ship with their belongings, I noticed that when some beans fell, they all crouched down to pick them up as if one of their eyes had fallen out."[3]

Christopher Columbus was too sick to accompany his men on their expedition to the mainland, where they landed near what is now the port of Trujillo, naming the point of land *Caxinas*, the Arawak name for a tree they found there. Mass was said, and on September 12 the expedition sailed further south, rounding with difficulty the cape they called *Gracias a Dios*, the name today of the most eastern department of Honduras. The name "Honduras" (in Spanish it means "depths") supposedly originated from the prayers of thanks uttered by Columbus when his ships had at last rounded the cape, escaping a tricky storm and heading south: "Thanks be to God we have got out of these depths".

The shock of conquest

After Columbus came the conquistadores, avid seekers of gold and slaves to work in the Caribbean sugar plantations. Their effect upon the Indian population was disastrous. Although the figures provided by demographic historians vary, all reveal a rapid decline in the Indian population due to massacres, enslavement, overwork, and disease. For centuries, a labour shortage was one of Honduras's chief problems. By the mid-1980s there were barely forty-three thousand native people left, most of them descendants of the Lenca people on the western border, or Payas, Sumus, and Miskitos living along the border with Nicaragua.[4]

The number of Spanish settlers was surprisingly small in the first years following the conquest, as it was in all Spanish possessions. Trujillo, the largest town in Honduras in 1547, had no more than fifty Spaniards; in fact, the total number of Spaniards in Honduras at that time was only two hundred.[5] But the decline in numbers of the native people astounded even the Governor, Francisco de Montejo. In 1539 the Governor wrote to the King of Spain about the town of Taiva, which once had four hundred houses: "But when I came there I found five and thirty men and no more than forty houses. And Cárcamo had once had five hundred and now has twenty. Araxagua, two hundred and fifty and now has forty. Yopoa two hundred and seventy and now has thirty. Lepaera four hundred and now has only seventy or eighty."[6]

Epidemics preceded the conquistadores. The smallpox, influenza, measles, and bubonic plague that they brought to the Caribbean reached Meso-America ahead of them. And because disease and overwork had decimated the native Caribbean population, Indians in Honduras were seized and carried off to island sugar plantations to provide a new labour force.

As early as 1516 boatloads of Honduran Indians were exported. The chronicler Antonio de Herrera reported on the adventures of one group of slaves who turned the tables on their Spanish masters in 1516. When the boat reached Havana, most of the Spaniards disembarked to celebrate a successful voyage. The Indians freed themselves, killed the guards, hoisted sail, and without maps or compass returned safely to Honduras.[7]

Christopher Columbus began the use of Indians as trade goods. He sent shipments of Indian slaves back to Spain, explaining, in 1495, that the shipment was "to compensate for the financial sacrifices entailed by the expeditions on the high seas".[8] But the enslavement of Indians for labour became so widespread that another governor of Honduras, Andrés de Cereceda, complained in 1548: "They have taken to Peru more than six thousand free Indians, selling them as slaves; in this manner they have depopulated this coast."[9]

The very last thing that Spain wanted was the depopulation of its Central American colonies. It needed a sizeable local population to work the mines and plantations and pay tribute. The Spanish crown was also wary of allowing the rise of a class of feudal lords independent of royal authority. The church, too, was interested in preserving enough Indians to construct churches and provide service to the priests. But the Spanish authorities were also preoccupied with justification for their Indian policy. The Pope had "given" Spain rights of conquest in the Americas, but there was a legal preoccupation with the doctrinal foundations of Indian enslavement. Did the Indians have souls, for instance? It would be convenient to find a religious justification that would fit the interests of both the Spanish crown and the Spanish settlers whose motives for sailing to the new world were purely mercenary.

Francisco de Montejo, Governor in 1536, admitted:

Many of the conquerors and settlers and other persons who have come and gone had no intention of staying or of populating the country, but of acquiring quantities of gold and silver and returning with it to Spain or of going further.

And so not only have our plans for population been hindered, but the result has been the bad treatment of the Indians.[10]

More to satisfy the royal conscience than as a serious way to solve this problem, the Spanish crown had a document drawn up which the conquistadores were supposed to read to the Indians before any attack. This *requerimiento* or "requirement" stated in part:

If you do not [submit to God and to Spain], or if you maliciously delay in so doing, I swear that with God's help I will advance powerfully against you and make war on you wherever and however I am able and will subject you to the yoke, to obedience to the Church and their majesties, and take your women and children to be slaves, and as such I will sell and dispose of them as their majesties may order, and I will take your possessions and do you all the harm and damage that I can.[11]

Bartolomé de las Casas, a former colonist turned friar, protested that he did not know whether to laugh or weep on reading this "requirement". He argued that the only way to win souls and to create a Christian empire was by peaceful colonization. His entreaties gained the ear of the Spanish crown, but not entirely for humanitarian reasons. Spain feared that unbridled colonial feudalism might threaten its own power and divert the riches anticipated from the new world. Whoever controlled Indian labour would be the masters, and the crown was not going to abdicate control, however difficult it might be to enforce it.

Labour control

Authority over the Indian population was administered through the *encomienda* system, which transferred the crown's right of tribute to an individual as a reward for service. So the Spanish generals rewarded their lieutenants and established some form of limit to the traditional system of looting and plunder. The *encomendero*, as agent of the crown, was responsible for the Indians' education, defence, and security. All Indians were forbidden to carry arms, while the Spaniards were obliged to defend the colony.

In Honduras, the number of Indians parcelled out among *encomenderos* was not large. For example, in the city of Trujillo there were only 197 Indians serving a handful of *encomenderos*.[12] What had begun as a system of tribute, developing into a system of labour control, was not working. The severe decline in the population made *encomiendas* unprofitable, because the *encomendero* was supposed to support a parish priest and pay heavy taxes out of the dwindling tribute he collected from the Indians in his control. There were not enough Indians to provide either labour or wealth.

The New Laws of the Indies, decreed in 1542, announced an end to the *encomienda* system, abolishing Indian enslavement and decreeing the existing *encomiendas* lapsed on the death of the *encomendero*. In practice, however, many of the *encomiendas* continued in Central America until well into the seventeenth century.

The new system, *repartimiento*, applied to all the adult male Indian population, not just to those directly allotted to a settler; therefore it increased not only the labour supply but the tribute that the colonies paid to Spain. Each Indian had to provide a certain amount of time, in rotation, for labour on ranches, in mines, and on public works, receiving a token wage. Both the *encomienda* and the *repartimiento* systems were disguised slavery; the essential difference was the rise in tribute paid to Spain – from one hundred thousand Mexican pesos in 1550 to more than one million a year by the end of the eighteenth century.[13]

Repartimiento, in turn, gave way later to debt servitude, as the Spanish colonists developed ranches and mines that needed a dependable labour supply. Indians were lured as paid workers, and held by the debts they owed for housing and food. Sometimes they were given a small plot of land, but at other times they lived like prisoners, kept away from their families for years. The expansion of the ranches with use of such labour had two further results: it thwarted any effort by the Spanish crown to provide Indians with opportunities to become full-fledged citizens of the kingdom; and it led to major confrontations between Indians and Spaniards, as the new forms of production clashed with the feudal power of Indian leaders who were ready to defend traditional Indian lands to the death.

Indian rebellion

Lempira, known to his thirty thousand warriors as "Lord of the Mountains", led continuous rebellions against Pedro de Alvarado's Spanish forces between 1537 and 1539. The sixteenth-century Spanish chronicler Antonio de Herrera described him as "of medium height, broad-shouldered and thick-limbed, fierce and courageous and of high intelligence. He never had more than two women and he was killed when he was between 38 and 39."[14] Lempira came to rule an empire of over 300 square miles and is said to have killed 120 men in battle.

The most likely story of his immediate motive for rebellion concerns the deaths of some of his people at the hands of Indians brought by Pedro de Alvarado from Mexico. Lempira and two other leaders were arrested when they retaliated. Sentenced to be hanged, Lempira escaped and fled to the mountains of western Honduras, where he united hitherto warring tribes in common cause and became the lord of two hundred Indian villages. According to Herrera's account:

This Indian, called Lempira, called on all the Indian warriors within the territory.... He persuaded them to fight for their freedom, since it was a shameful thing that so many and so valiant men, within their own lands, were obliged to live in miserable servitude to a handful of foreigners. He offered to be their captain and to risk the greatest dangers; he was convinced that, if they were united, victory would be certain.[15]

Lempira made his stand at the settlement of Cerquín, holding out against the Spaniards for six months, with bows and arrows against guns. Captain Alonso de Cáceres, deciding that trickery was the only way to defeat Lempira, ordered a soldier to ride up to a rock where the leader was standing and offer peace negotiations. Another soldier, hidden, aimed his gun at the Indian chief. Lempira is reported to have replied to the peace overtures "with arrogant words, saying that war ought not to weary soldiers or frighten them and that he who had the greatest strength could emerge the victor".

The hidden Spaniard took aim and hit Lempira in the forehead. "It mattered not that he was wearing his splendid war helmet with its plumes," writes Herrera. Lempira fell "turning over and over down the mountainside".[16]

As the Indian population declined, the first African slaves were brought in. Whatever might have been the Spaniards' squeamishness about enslaving Indians, there was general agreement that blacks were children of the devil and therefore fair game. Many Spanish officials brought black slaves with them as personal servants. More arrived from Santo Domingo to work the gold and silver mines, and by 1545 Honduras had fifteen hundred African slaves.

Black slaves were considered a bad influence on the Indians, and any communication between the races was forbidden, as a Crown decree stated, "because the Blacks are very harmful to the Indians, encouraging them in drinking, in vice, in bad habits, in stealing and in many other mischiefs".[17] Punishment for black slaves was harsh: fifty lashes for escape and four days' absence from work, or hanging for absence of more than six months.

Two Spanish priests reported the aptness of Indian retribution in 1608, after a Lenca Indian being punished for striking a Commander in the face was nailed to a tree by his hand, his other hand roped to his side, and was left to die. His companions found him dead and sent a message to the priests who accompanied the Spanish forces, saying they wanted to be baptised. They asked the priests to come to them unarmed. Anticipating a trick of some sort, the priests consulted with the Spanish captain, who decided to go himself. The Indians ambushed him and nailed him to a tree with the same eight nails taken from the palm of their dead companion.[18]

Spanish rivalries: boom and bust

Trouble with Indians and slaves was a minor irritation compared to the serious rivalry among the conquistadores. The conflicts led to a kind of social chaos that slowed development throughout colonial rule.

Competitors for power in Honduras came north from Panama, south from Mexico and west from the Caribbean, and for years it was not clear where Honduras fitted into the Spanish empire. Vasco Núñez de Balboa, conqueror of Panama and famed for being the first white man to see the Pacific, was appointed to be the first governor of Honduras but was killed before he could leave Panama. His appointed successor landed from Santo Domingo only to find a rival, from Mexico, already in possession. The resultant squabble had to be settled by Hernán Cortés, conqueror of Mexico, who came to Honduras after hacking his way through the Guatemalan jungle for six months, with the deposed Aztec emperor in tow as a hostage. Cortés finally set up his cousin, Hernando de Saavedra, as governor of Honduras in 1526.

The Spanish crown did not help matters with its inability to decide where the seat of power for Central America should be placed. Honduras was first choice, with Gracias, a gold-mining centre in western Honduras, chosen in 1544. When the gold ran out, the *audiencia* – seat of colonial government – was moved to Panama and then to Santiago in Guatemala. Honduras was downgraded into a mayoralty rather than a governorship, until silver deposits were discovered at Tegucigalpa in 1578, giving it a renewed importance. The colonial authorities responded by creating not one but two Honduran provinces – one based in Comayagua and one in Tegucigalpa; Honduran authority was not truly united until 1788.[19]

The boom and bust in gold, and later silver, were symptomatic of Honduran luck with export resources. In the mid-sixteenth century, teams of hundreds of Indians and African slaves washed gold from the streams; one river, the Guaypo near Olancho in the eastern part of Honduras, produced nearly two million Mexican pesos of gold in ten years.[20] But the ore ran out, and so did the labour.

Cattle were brought in to feed the miners and turned out to be the next resource. A trade in hides and tallow developed, but was never lucrative. Spanish settlers continued to search for a new export crop, one that would require little labour and take up little space on ships back to Spain, which held a monopoly of trade. First came balsam, an unguent extracted from trees and advertised as a cure for all medical ills. Then there was sarsaparilla, made from dried roots and used as a tonic against fever. There were indigo, a bush used for blue dye, and cochineal, a red dye made from an unlikely source, insect wings. Honduran colonists tried them all, but neighbouring nations were in competition and the market in Europe was limited.

Cacao was a much more popular export, as Europeans acquired a taste for drinking chocolate. But cacao grew best on the slopes of the Pacific coast and needed expert labour and easy access to ports, none of which Honduras could provide.[21]

Piracy on the Caribbean coast discouraged trade and made mining even more difficult: mercury was needed for smelting, and the only sources were Spain or Peru. Miners often had to wait years for a shipment of mercury.[22] The silver mines around Tegucigalpa proved difficult to operate without pumps, due to the high water-table, and the declining mineral production had serious effects upon the social development of the country. Ambitious settlers simply moved on; the less ambitious settled into life on the *hacienda*, overseeing the raising of a few cattle and taking little interest in national development. Subsistence agriculture became the basis of the country's economy until at least the latter part of the nineteenth century.

Lack of exports meant a further decline in the ports. For over a decade in the seventeenth century, not one ship put into the Gulf of Honduras.[23] The main port of Trujillo declined. Puerto Caballos, a little further west, proved dangerous to shipping because of local marine parasites that destroyed wooden ships. So few new settlers arrived that, between the seventeenth and eighteenth centuries, more Africans than Europeans came to Honduras to live.

Another factor in the decay of colonial rule was the absence of any central-ized power, due to the division of power between Tegucigalpa and Comay-agua. Greedy landowners squabbled over land, with no institution to restrain them. There was not even the power of the church, as in neighbouring Guate-mala, since the church in Honduras was as poor and as sparsely scattered as the population. By the end of the eighteenth century, Honduras had less than one-third the number of churches that Guatemala had.

Held back by isolation and poverty, Honduras did not open its first college until 1787 (Guatemala had a university in 1676). Although Guatemala had a printing press in 1660, the first Honduran newspaper did not appear until 1829, the first book in 1836, and the first bookstore in 1850 (even that was owned by a French citizen). There were no public schools until the late 1850s.[24]

The empire disintegrates

Spanish colonial policy restricted regional trade in order to favour the mother-country: the practice of mercantilism. But Honduran trade with Spain was threatened by pirate attacks and British incursions. The British captured Havana in 1762, seeking to supplant the weakened Spanish Carib-bean empire. They established settlements to the north of Honduras in what became known as British Honduras (now Belize), and to the south on the east-ern coast of Nicaragua and in Panama. Although fewer than fifteen hundred British immigrants settled on the Caribbean coast in the eighteenth century, ladino descendants of Indians and whites swelled the population.

Britain encouraged the establishment of the Kingdom of Mosquitia, partly in Honduras and partly in Nicaraguan territory. In 1687 the British Governor of Jamaica crowned a Miskito chief as King Jeremy I. Throughout his reign, which lasted until 1723, King Jeremy led the Miskitos in raids on Spanish forts, using bows and poisoned arrows. In 1702, attacks reached San Pedro Sula, inland on the other side of Honduras. British raiders deflected a Spanish flotilla in Honduran waters in 1723, with all but nine of the 180 aboard losing their lives. Raiders went further south in 1750, capturing and executing the Spanish governor of Costa Rica. Encouraged by the 1779 war between Britain and Spain, British navy ships attacked and destroyed Fort Omoa, a fort that had taken the Hondurans twenty-five years to build.

The British also took a firm hold on the nearby islands in the Caribbean Sea. In 1650, a Spanish commander took four warships and chased British squatters off the main island of Roatán. Nevertheless, the British returned and used the island as a base for further incursions, even though Britain renounced its claims by a peace treaty signed in 1783. Spain was too busy with European wars to defend or develop its Central American possessions adequately, although the eighteenth-century Bourbon kings did attempt some colonial reforms and lifted the embargo on inter-colonial trade.

By 1800 the days of Spain's traditional empire were over, and Britain's economic and political empire was on the rise, as the industrial revolution increased the demand for overseas resources and markets. The bankruptcy of the Spanish empire is best shown by the fact that barely sixty pesos were left in the *audiencia*'s treasury in Guatemala City in 1821. Nowhere was the weakness of Spanish colonialism more apparent than in Honduras. Rafael Heliodoro Valle, a Honduran historian, commented on the social, economic, cultural and political neglect: "If any country in America were to demonstrate the bad policies of Spain ... it would be Honduras."[25]

Honduras, more so than other colonies, was left utterly unprepared for the nineteenth-century movement towards independence in the region. It was without a government infrastructure, a stable, established economy, or any sense of national integration. Spanish rule provided a dubious preparation for what lay ahead.

4

Independence and Civil War

"Central American independence made every village a sovereign state."
DOMINGO FAUSTINO SARMIENTO,
Argentinian historian and president 1874-88

In Central America the movement for independence in the early nineteenth century had little to do with nationhood and still less with the class struggle, at least as it is commonly understood. The disputes were, rather, a struggle for power between the *criollos*, colonists of Spanish ancestry born in Central America, and the *peninsulares*, who were born in Spain and favoured with official positions in the colonial empire.

Indians and ladinos – those of mixed Spanish and Indian blood – outnumbered them both, twenty to one, but were left totally outside the realm of political life. The Indians were considered *gente sin razón* (people without intelligence) and Indian-Spanish offspring were not as readily accepted in Central America as elsewhere in the empire.[1] Ladinos were mistrusted by both *criollos* and *peninsulares* and, like Indians, were forbidden to carry firearms or even knives.[2] Ladinos became farmers and small merchants, if they were lucky, drifters and thieves if they were not. Their future generations would eventually form the middle classes, but they did not gain political power until they had acquired some economic power, a century later.

The *criollo* sons of wealthy Spaniards, on the other hand, had land and economic influence but were barred from administrative positions except in local government. Towards the end of the eighteenth century, however, the Spanish government opened up lower-rung bureaucratic posts to the *criollos* and encouraged them to form merchant guilds. But by that time, feelings between *criollos* and *peninsulares* had reached danger levels. *Criollos* were boasting, "I am not a Spaniard. I am an American" or even vowing to empty their veins of Spanish blood.[3]

The *peninsulares* continued to be the only class with access to the Spanish court and closely guarded their privileges. They looked down on the *criollos* as indolent spendthrifts who had become vitiated by the enervating Central American climate. In return, the *criollos* called the *peninsulares* "*gachupines*" or tenderfeet, and eyed them as Johnny-come-latelies who knew nothing about the land they had come to govern.

Jealousies between different groups of Spaniards – Castilians against Andalusians, for instance – added to the hostilities in the region. Other rivalries grew between the Spanish-born aristocracies in the outer provinces and the *peninsulares* who held power in the seat of the Spanish *audiencia,* Guatemala City. Both *peninsulares* and *criollos* exploited the complex web of envy and ambition. They fought over access to power in any new form of government, over state control of the church, and over the issue of free trade rather than over the principle of independence.

Elsewhere in South America, the independence movement had begun as early as 1810, with riots, demonstrations, and declarations of independence first in Venezuela and later in Ecuador, Argentina, Chile, Peru, and Bolivia. The movement was not merely aimed at independence, but for a republican form of government and for confederation. Simón Bolívar, liberator of South America, even considered a confederation of all American nations.

José Cecilio del Valle, the Honduran who wrote the first Central American constitution, recognized the new force of the growing movement for political change:

The north of America began to move in 1774 and by declaring itself independent of English government, gave a lesson to Mexico and Guatemala, and to Chile and Buenos Aires. France erupted in 1789, and, shedding light on her own children and those of all the world, defended its freedom and taught men how to defend their own.[4]

But the Central American states never fought for their independence; they fought about it, and if revolution had not begun elsewhere first, it might never have begun in Central America.

Discussion, not revolution

Independence began with a debating society, not a revolutionary cell. Significantly, the first president of the *Sociedad Económica de Amigos del País* (Economic Society of Friends of the Nation), founded in Guatemala City in

1795, was no youthful revolutionary, but a ninety-six-year old scholar. The society's aim was merely "to promote and encourage agriculture, industry, the arts and businesses of the kingdom by means of discussions, demonstrations, prizes and such things as are accustomed in the societies of Europe".[5] The references to discussion and Europe were the only indications of a move towards free thought; the Spanish Inquisition's ban on reading Rousseau, Voltaire, or even Erasmus extended also to the Spanish empire. The authorities suppressed the Society in 1800, giving notice that they recognized the subversive potential in its lectures on political economy.

The Society did manage to get one of its members elected to the legislative assembly set up by Napoleon in Spain. The delegate was sent to Spain to press for colonial reform, but had barely arrived and signed, with some others, "instructions" demanding reform when King Ferdinand was returned to power. Ferdinand, who had been imprisoned by Napoleon, was understandably upset by what he considered premature enthusiasm for freedom: "His Majesty is convinced that the aforementioned instructions, in which many propositions from the National Assembly in France were copied to the letter, have been the flame that has lit the torch of discord in our countries."[6]

The Central American delegate and others who had signed "instructions" were banned from public office for life. But there was no way the revived Spanish monarchy could stop the pressure for reform. Insurrections broke out in San Salvador and in Granada, Nicaragua, in 1811. In Tegucigalpa in 1812, *criollos* from both that town and Comayaguela marched to the main plaza armed with sticks and machetes and accompanied by the parish priest. They surrounded the houses of the Spanish authorities and demanded a share in government; the insurrection was repressed by loyal troops.

Church repression

These abortive revolts intensified the paranoia of the provincial governor, who called the protesters monsters and heretics and accused them of plotting to behead priests, rape nuns, and desecrate altars. José Bustamante y Guerra, the governor in Guatemala, demanded that the rebels be expelled from society "as a father of the family dismisses a disruptive servant".[7] The Archbishop of Guatemala also fulminated against the protesters, calling them a "nest of vipers" attempting to shake off the "gentle yoke of God's divine law and of Spanish dominion".[8] This sort of attack encouraged a backlash of anticlerical reforms in Central America's final declaration of independence, which stripped all bishops and archbishops of any title except "padre". Church privilege was to become a bone of contention thereafter.

In Mexico, independence came about through a conservative reaction against peasant uprisings and against the new, liberal monarchy in Spain. Agustín de Iturbide took power in 1820, and announced separation from Spain through the Plan of Iguala. Two years later, he proclaimed himself emperor and invited the Central American provinces to join his empire. The debate about Central American independence therefore became one of whether to join Mexico or to pronounce a separate form of independence from Spain.

Apart from ladino protests against the privileges of the Spanish-born, the desire for independence in the Central American provinces stemmed more from economic dissatisfaction than any desire for sovereignty. Spanish monopoly of trade had caused economic hard times at the end of the eighteenth century. Even inter-provincial trade depended upon European markets. For example, the Honduran farmers who provided cattle and grain to the indigo plantations in Guatemala and El Salvador lost their markets when the European demand for indigo fell. Many Central American *criollos* wanted a new export system that would allow access to other markets, and so they would support whatever type of government favoured their interests, whether this meant joining the Mexican empire or total independence.

The pressure they exerted on provincial governors forced a meeting of the Guatemalan City Council and the provincial deputies with the Spanish Captain General in Guatemala City, 1821. It was decided to prepare a document of independence. The Honduran José Cecilio del Valle, who was empowered to draw up the document, was so uncertain of its reception that he declined to sign it.

The issue of joining or not joining Mexico was not even mentioned. The document merely called for establishment of a Congress that would decide how independence should come about. The Guatemalan conservative leader Mariano de Aycinena made it quite clear why his supporters signed: it was to prevent "consequences that would be fearful should the people themselves proclaim independence".[9]

The issue of annexation to Mexico divided every state of the proposed union, and led to a wave of regional and local conflicts. Within Honduras, Comayagua, the more conservative centre, favoured annexation; Tegucigalpa, the more liberal, opposed it, and the two cities went to war. Agustín de Iturbide, self-styled Emperor of Mexico, threatened to send troops into Central America to force its annexation. When Cecilio del Valle was called to Mexico to help write a Central American constitution, he found himself writing it in jail, where he spent six months until Iturbide was deposed and later executed when he attempted a return to power in 1823. It was therefore Mexican pressure and resultant political confusion, rather than any Central American accord, that brought the states together and allowed signing of complete Central American independence as "The United Provinces of the Center of America", on July 1, 1823.

Cecilio del Valle drew up a constitution, the following year, which declared each state free and independent in all its governmental and internal administration. A federal congress would legislate matters of common interest and federal taxes. Individual states were expected to contribute to cover the federal deficit. It was a curious mixture of the Spanish Constitution of 1812 and the U.S. Constitution of 1789. It guaranteed Roman Catholicism as the exclusive religion of state, outlawed slavery, and established a congress that could override senate vetoes and a president with no veto power at all.

It called for a constituent assembly elected by each state according to proportional representation, and a senate consisting of two representatives from each state. Government at state level would be on a similar pattern, with the federal authority retaining control over criminal, civil, and commercial law – a more nationalist approach than in the United States constitution of 1789.

The provision of guarantees for Catholicism as the exclusive state religion, and the outlawing of slavery ensured support of both conservatives and reformers, but division arose immediately among the states over election of a federal president, with the more radical Salvadoran liberal, Manuel José de Arce, defeating Del Valle. There was also intense conflict over where the seat of federal authority should be. The more southern states ganged up against Guatemala, the traditional seat of power, the centre of conservatism and by far the most powerful state. In 1820 Guatemala had nearly 50 per cent of the total Central American population of little more than a million people. Honduras had a population of less than two hundred thousand.

It was all very well for a foreign liberator, Simón Bolívar, to imagine a confederation of states from Panama to Guatemala, made so rich by the attraction of a trans-isthmus canal that all nations would establish a seat of world government in that "happy region".[10] The realities were very different.

To begin with, very little change was apparent to Central American peasants, who were not encouraged to hope for any. In fact, the provincial governor of Honduras even prohibited the ringing of bells to celebrate Central American independence, in case it should generate mass enthusiasm. The small European-based population – only 4 per cent of the total – was in control.

Gradually, the heat of debate engendered two major political parties, at least in embryo. Reformers favouring a North American type of confederation became known as Liberals. They tended to be middle-class ladinos from the outer provinces or from provincial Guatemala; their political principles ranged from vague ideals about progress to a more mundane interest in the profits to be gained through free trade. The Conservatives were largely upper-class *creoles* with respect for the church and basic tradition, a fear of reform, and a desire for a more centralized union along the old colonial lines.[11]

As soon as they took power in 1824, the Liberals began a flood of reforms, ending slavery and colonial taxes, encouraging immigration from other European countries, and limiting monopolies. Some reforms were premature and others were not viable without a stable economy and ready cash; the new Union had neither.

Lack of funds led to a series of crippling loans from a London bank. This reliance on foreign financing and foreign concepts of progress stirred up Conservative resentment and frightened away Liberal moderates, like Manuel José Arce, the Union's first president. Two years after taking office, he went over to the Conservative side, and marched into Honduras to put down a rebellion led by Liberal President Dionisio de Herrera. It was Arce's repression of liberalism in Honduras in 1826 that brought in the man who would become the champion of Central American unity: Francisco Morazán.

Francisco Morazán

The hero of Central American union was a *criollo*, born to parents of Corsican and Spanish descent in Tegucigalpa on October 3, 1789. He learned grammar, mathematics, history, and drafting from a friar and taught himself French in order to read Rousseau's *Social Contract*. He worked first as a law clerk and later for the city government at the time when Tegucigalpa and Comayagua took up arms over whether to join Mexico or declare a separate union.

Morazán, just twenty-two, was captured as a spy by the forces of Comayagua, but managed to talk his way free. He joined the staff of Dionisio de Herrera, president of the first Honduran constituent assembly, and a Liberal reformer. But de Herrera was under vicious attack by the Guatemalan Archbishop Ramón Casaus, who had de Herrera's library burned, denounced him to the Pope, and finally had him deposed. Morazán fought in the ensuing battle, was held prisoner for ten days, and barely escaped with his life to Nicaragua. When he returned the following year, 1827, it was at the head of an army that would defeat the foes of Liberalism.

Morazán, the statesman, would continually have to take up arms to defend his policies and ideals. Between 1827 and 1840, he fought twenty-one battles, some lasting as long as twenty-eight days. He won all but his last fight against the Guatemalan *caudillo* Rafael Carrera, in Guatemala City, 1840.

Latin Americans venerate Morazán as a Central American military and political leader to rival Napoleon:

Napoleon took advantage of existing conditions; Morazán created those conditions because there was nothing on which to build.

The ideas of Bonaparte were those of France; those of Morazán were not shared and the struggle had to begin from the beginning.

Napoleon sought his own aggrandisement; Morazán exclusively that of his country.

Napoleon believed only in force and used it throughout his life; Morazán recognized only the force of right and used his army to secure institutions.

Napoleon conquered; Morazán stretched out the bonds of union and cut the abuses of the past.[12]

Most modern historians agree on Morazán's military genius, but not on the characterization of Morazán as a hero of democracy.[13] Some would argue that Morazán's liberalism was an artificial, western approach that merely opened the way to foreign investment at the expense of local development. This argument covers the much larger question of what constitutes progress. To the Liberal reformers who took power with Morazán, it meant modernization on European or North American lines, under a capitalist economic system, using foreign capital to transform what was basically a feudal mode of production. The Conservatives opposed such reforms in order to protect their own interests and those of the Church. Incidentally, Conservative policies also protected some of the traditional freedoms of the rural population, especially the indigenous people.

Although history has honoured Morazán as representing the light of liberty and the spirit of union, his Liberal reforms were not in fact lasting ones. Too many were imported, and too few arose from popular demand or need. His substitution of North American practices for those of the old colonial system included public education, freedom of worship, abolition of church tithes, and institution of a direct head tax to pay for new roads and harbours. He promoted industry, immigration, and commerce, and organized a diplomatic service and a judicial system. The new president of the Central American Federation appeared to the outside world as a Latin George Washington. But his reforms alarmed many of his subjects, not just the hide-bound clergy. One example was the Livingstone Code of penal reform, which was imported wholesale from Louisiana and proved to be totally confusing to Guatemalans, who had no history of trial by jury.[14] The code also contemplated a more humane jail system, but natives conscripted to build model jails had difficulty seeing this as reform.

Opposition to Morazán

Morazán made enemies in the church by seizing church funds, censoring church correspondence, suppressing monastic orders, and exiling dissident clergy. Father José Trinidad Reyes, Honduras's first poet, objected strongly when Morazán exiled the dissident Archbishop of Guatemala, Ramón Casaus.

The landowning elite objected to reforms that encouraged colonization by Northern Europeans and a system of small holdings. The native chiefs also felt their communal landholdings threatened. Faced with rising opposition to reform, Morazán was forced to use more repressive tactics that seemed to contradict his Liberal principles.

The crisis came when a cholera epidemic struck Guatemala in 1837 and government troops enforced a quarantine. Both Indians and ladinos, led by their priests, refused to submit to the measure. Their resistance found a leader in José Rafael Carrera, a ladino peasant with firm roots in the Indian community. In addition to mass support, Carrera also had the encouragement of some radical Liberals as well as the Conservatives – a support that would enable him to dominate Central American politics for twenty-five years after the fall of Morazán.

Many Indians saw Carrera as their saviour, but to the Guatemala City aristocracy he was a "barbarian". U.S. agent John Lloyd Stephens described him as "ignorant, fanatic, sanguinary and the slave to violent passions, wielding absolutely the physical force of the country and that force entertaining a natural hatred of the whites".[15]

Carrera entered Guatemala City on February 1, 1838, at the head of an army, taking over the capital and beginning a series of conflicts that was to break up the Central American Federation. It is possible that the gradual reforms he advocated might have brought more benefits to peasants in the long run. Or perhaps, given time, Morazán's reforms would have been implemented with more consideration. But Morazán did not have time. He was continually occupied at putting down attacks upon the union.

The other states were jealous because Guatemala occupied so much of Morazán's attention. When he tried to combat this resentment by moving the federal administration to El Salvador, the other states protested, each wanting special advantages and refusing to share power. Recognizing this fragmentation, Morazán pressed for the building of a trans-isthmus canal that would be a United Province's project rather than that of one state or some foreign power, and would therefore encourage unity.

But the Central American states did not share his dream. As historian Mario Rodríguez writes about the Nicaragua of that time: "If there was any consciousness of Central Americanism in Nicaragua, it was nothing more than an oratorical device."[16] The same could be said for every other nation of Central America.

Union was also opposed by Frederick Chatfield, Britain's agent in Central America from 1834 to 1852, who saw it as a threat to British ambitions along the Caribbean coast. But Chatfield's opposition was an additional rather than a motivating force in the break-up. Rivalry between the states, lack of experience in self-government (a legacy of colonial domination), greed, and the lack of a general commitment to reform and united policy-making doomed both liberalism and Central American union to failure.

By the end of 1839, Costa Rica, Honduras, Nicaragua, and Guatemala (except for the Los Altos province) had seceded. Union was dead. Morazán left his headquarters and El Salvador and sailed for Peru, where he considered, but later declined, offers to lead the Peruvian army against Chile – another squabble arising from the degeneration of Bolívar's dreams.

John Lloyd Stephens commented: "I verily believe they have driven from their shores the best man in Central America."[17]

Two years after he left, Morazán was back, leading a Liberal coup against a Conservative government in Costa Rica as part of a plan to re-create Central American union. Shortly after, he was in turn overthrown in a counter-revolution and captured by the Costa Rican loyalist troops. The story goes that he was given permission to command his own execution, that he said "Ahora, bien ... fuego!" but that the first volley failed to kill him. He was heard to say "Estoy vivo!" – "I am alive!" – before a second discharge ended his life.[18] He died on September 15, 1842, the anniversary of Central American independence.

Morazán was a martyr to the ideals he espoused and tried to engender in a region unprepared for change – a region described as nothing more than "a league of towns, suspicious of each other and linked only by common concern for protection".[19] John Lloyd Stephens blamed Morazán's failure on his antagonization of the church. Chatfield questioned the ability of "Spanish-Indian" races to govern themselves at all, with or without Liberalism.

Morazán's accomplishments have been both overpraised and denied. Although he relied on the popular masses in his many battles, he was, nevertheless, not an advocate of popular government or democracy as we know it; he was, rather, a Liberal reformer. It was his faith in Central American unity that made him unique.

When he died, so did belief in unity. The states would come together again briefly, in 1865, to defeat a common enemy, the Yankee "filibuster" William Walker. After Walker was routed, the states went their separate ways; subsequent unity proposals would never get far beyond the planning stage. Likewise, Morazán's Liberal reforms were overturned by Conservative regimes throughout the region. The church regained its power; the economies stagnated.

Honduras suffered more than any of the other Central American states from the defeat of Morazán and – with him – the ideals of liberalism and Central American union. Because of Morazán, Honduras had enjoyed a sense of reflected glory. Many of its best citizens had fought in his campaigns but many, too, had lost their lives, leaving a power vacuum within the thin ranks of the Honduran elite.

Nor did Honduras have a strong Conservative alternative to take the place of a Liberal government and provide stability. With the fall of Morazán, Honduras was to sink into almost a century of civil strife that set back any hope of economic progress and left, instead, a nation vulnerable to outside influence at a crucial time in its battered history.

5

The Age of Adventurism

"This parcel of independent little states is a constant danger to the peace which should exist between great powers."

RICHARD HARDING DAVIS, 1896

The failure of Central American unity added one more unhappy experience in the chain of Honduran misfortunes. So little national spirit was left that Honduras meekly acknowledged the British rights to the Kingdom of Mosquitia and even asked Guatemala to take over all Honduran diplomatic and commercial functions overseas.

From 1842 to 1876, Honduras suffered economic stagnation, social decline, and arbitrary government. Disillusioned with central government, Morazán's lieutenants retired to isolated fiefdoms, beginning a Honduran tradition that still calls a landowner "colonel" and accepts local, feudal rule more readily than centralized government. For years to come, Honduras was to have two types of general: the one officially appointed by government and the other *general gritado*, self-appointed or literally "shouted", who ran his own small army and was responsible to no one. Conservative governments took over in all the Central American states, but in Honduras they were unable to promote stability, let alone Morazán's version of Western liberalism.

Now that Spanish power had faded, Western nations were taking an interest in Central America and, because of its proximity to the Caribbean, Honduras was the first country eyed. The British government saw in Honduras the key to an empire across the Pacific as well as a useful buffer for British possessions and claims in the Caribbean and Mosquitia. The United States, for its part, was in the process of buying off French, Spanish, and Russian claims to North American territory, and anxious to secure its western coast following the discovery of gold in California.

By the mid-nineteenth century Central America had something else to offer to the bigger powers anxious to extend and defend their empires: the possibility of a trans-isthmus canal linking the Pacific and Atlantic oceans. It was a time for the Central American states to bargain and grow rich, perhaps. Instead, each of them was outsmarted by bidders. As a Central American federation, they might have been able to withstand the adroit diplomacy, sharp trading, and less than veiled threats of Britain and the United States. As individual, impoverished, and inexperienced states, they sold cheap and bought dear, opening their territories to unprincipled foreigners and beginning a process by which Honduras was to become a nation for rent.

Although the Central American states owned land that could be used for a canal, they lacked the financial resources to undertake such a project themselves. They wanted – and needed – to sell just as earnestly as the bigger powers wanted to buy, but in the end bad loans and unwise concessions opened the way to foreign domination. The regrets would come later, like this romantic lament, written a century too late (in 1954) by a Honduran politician:

If, instead of the infamous policy of concessions, we could have foreseen the effects of the invasion of foreign capital in the hands of greedy businessmen. If, instead of embarking on a continuing policy of granting concessions, some policy of protection had arisen, the Honduran of today would not be a mere labourer. From one end to the other of this privileged land there would be flourishing banana plantations for his exclusive use. Today's Hondurans would not only be rich, they would be worthy sons of a small but proud and sovereign country."[1]

Honduras was especially weak economically in comparison with Guatemala and El Salvador. Those countries had moved from reliance on dye products to the profitable export of coffee, while Honduran exporters were trying to make money from the sale of tallow and hides. The members of Honduras's landowning elite were isolated from each other geographically, and had no commercially profitable economic activity. They had therefore little incentive for assuming a major role in national economic progress.

Chatfield and the British mission

Because British merchants had taken over much of the Caribbean commerce originally in the hands of Spain, British diplomats acquired important influence over the newly independent states, and no other diplomat had the power of Frederick Chatfield, British agent from 1834 to 1852.

Chatfield represented the typical British concept of empire at the time, explained by the British Prime Minister, Lord Palmerston, as a noble mission to an inferior species: "an endeavour to import to a rude and barbarous Race of Men, some of the elements of social order, some rudiments of political organization and some instruction in the Truths of Religion".[2] Palmerston was referring to the aims of the British protectorate already set up on the Mosquito coast of Honduras and Nicaragua. Britain had captured a toe-hold on Honduran soil as early as 1642 by taking the island of Roatán. Eighteen years later, British woodcutters had settled on the shores of the Belize River, in what was to become British Honduras and later Belize. British pirates controlled much of the coast, even as far as Panama City, which Henry Morgan captured and burned in 1681. There was also the semi-official British interest in the Mosquito coast. When the Jamaica Governor crowned the Miskito Jeremy I as king, the act was meant to secure protection on the coast for British settlers.

For Honduras, as for Guatemala, Nicaragua, and Costa Rica, the influence of British traders and settlers over the native peoples would endanger national sovereignty, since it discouraged adherence to Latin American rule. The natives therefore proved useful to expansionist British foreign policy in the nineteenth century, just as they would to the U.S. campaign against Nicaragua in the 1980s.

Chatfield carefully orchestrated Britain's territorial claims in Central America. In the long term, a trans-isthmus canal was far more important than maintaining a few British loggers in a swamp on the Caribbean shore. However, their continued existence there gave Britain justification for attempting more far-reaching control – access to the eastern and western points of entry of a trans-isthmus canal – with the argument that it was merely protecting British territory.

Dreams of a canal

The idea of a trans-isthmus canal had originated as early as Spanish settlement, but became a serious project only after independence. In 1825, the United Provinces asked their national governments to survey their rivers, with an eye to an inter-oceanic route.

Nicaragua seemed to offer the most favourable conditions. The English engineer John Bailey surveyed a Nicaraguan route in 1837; both Dutch and U.S. companies made similar surveys. But the growing disharmony among the Central American states frightened away investors. Britain became convinced a canal would only be practical with British control over the entry points, making Honduras a better bet than Nicaragua. It would be easy to strengthen the British hold on the Caribbean, but more difficult to acquire access to Pacific land.

At first Chatfield was no enemy to Central American union. Tensions developed, however, when British settlers along the Belize river made repeated encroachments on Guatemalan territory. Soon these settlers were holding more than three times the area originally authorized; a strong and united Central American opponent did not make as much sense to Chatfield.

Another point of tension came when the United Provinces abolished slavery. Black slaves in British territory sought refuge across the river in Guatemala. The tension was sufficient for the United Provinces to send envoys to other European powers and to the United States seeking support against British territorial claims on their lands. But the states could not afford a direct confrontation with Britain. For one thing, they had contracted a huge debt to the British firm of Barclay, Herring and Richardson (a debt that would take fifty years to pay off). For another, British vessels had now taken over much of the import and export trade formerly carried in Spanish ships.

The "ominous Chatfield", the "eternal agent" as he was known, was not an easy man to bargain with. He was not seeking foreign popularity; rather, he liked to be considered tough. In a letter written in 1837, Chatfield wrote:

A residence in this Republic requires the patient relinquishment of the ordinary enjoyment of civilized life, while the political state of it places life and property in constant jeopardy; this is more particularly applicable to me, in consequence of the prevailing error that every person in the country who is not a Central American must be an Englishman, an error which goes to concentrating upon the English the whole weight of the antipathy which is commonly entertained against foreigners in rude and uncivilised countries.[3]

Chatfield had at first welcomed the Liberals' plans for foreign investment and European immigration, but became concerned by later programs of economic and social reform, and disenchanted with the lack of opportunities for British influence.

He began to establish relations with the Guatemalan Conservatives, and provided them with arms against Morazán. He began complex manoeuvres with the Conservatives in Nicaragua. He supported yet another in the series of British settlements on the island of Roatán in 1839. This last manoeuvre so angered the Guatemalans that the newspaper El Popular, published in Quetzaltenango, declaimed:

The important island of Roatán has been snatched away from us; practically all of the territory from Belize to El Petén has been usurped from us. A claim has been advanced to the entire country of the Mosquitos. The British consul, Chatfield, treats us with contempt and even insolence, which is unbearable to our patriotism ... this public enemy of America, advocate of the most anti-American and servile sentiments, special adversary of our nation and particularly and personally the foe of the Federal executive, has broken relations without notice.[4]

The humiliation of the Central American United Provinces continued even after Chatfield was recalled to Britain for consultation. The British superintendent of Belize undertook patrols of all British settlements, and kidnapped the commander of the port of San Juan, Nicaragua, on the pretext that the officer owed bills to British creditors. The British navy blockaded the Honduran coast until the post-Morazán government of Francisco Ferrera gave in and recognized British claims to the Kingdom of Mosquitia.

When Chatfield returned to Guatemala in 1844, his disruption of a tentative plan for another attempt at union so angered the various nations that he actually brought them together against him. They united to send a commission to Britain to demand his recall, but he stayed on.

There were continual accusations against him: that he put pressure on Costa Rica to break off talks with Honduras; that he was the chief obstacle to any federation of Central American states. He was an ideal scapegoat. Certainly he wanted to secure British control over the Central American Caribbean coast, whether it was by using British diplomacy, British loans, British trade, or British investment. British favour was crucial in Honduras, which had few resources beyond its mines (many of which had been sold to British investors) and its Caribbean trade (most of which was passing to Belize).

In the interests of U.S. peace and safety

The United States was at first not particularly interested in either Central American territory or Central American trade. It was concerned, however, about consolidating and protecting its own territory, about its sovereignty and the threat of European empires. That threat was embodied in the formation of the Holy Alliance, a group of European monarchies united against the spread of democracy, in Europe or anywhere in the world. When the Czar of Russia claimed sovereignty over the Pacific coast from what is now Alaska to the 51st parallel, the newly independent United States gave warning with the pronouncement of the Monroe Doctrine in 1823. President James Monroe declared that the American continents were:

henceforth not to be considered as subject for future colonization by any European powers.... We should consider any attempt on their part to extend their system to any portion of this hemisphere as dangerous to our peace and safety.[5]

Many additions were made to this Monroe Doctrine in attempts to justify growing aspirations for a U.S. economic empire. The doctrine has been both attacked as ruthless imperialism and praised as "the sheet-anchor of safety for storm-tossed republics".[6] Invoked as justification for U.S. hemispheric policy up to the present day, it denied the Latin American states neutrality and turned out in practice to provide a highly selective framework for protecting them from European powers. For example, when the new Argentinian nation protested Britain's reoccupation of the Falkland Islands in 1833, the United States refused to come to its aid.

The possibility of a canal aroused special U.S. interest in Central America. The first recommendation, given wide publicity by the explorer Alexander von Humboldt in 1805, had favoured a Honduran route. After seeing surveys prepared by the United Provinces, Morazán had favoured the Nicaraguan route.[7] The North American agent John Lloyd Stephens also investigated three possible routes (through Honduras, Panama, and Nicaragua) and came to the same conclusion as Morazán. A canal through Nicaragua, could, he said, be built for $25 million.

As soon as he learned of Stephens' investigations, Frederick Chatfield, still Britain's voice in Central America, moved fast to secure the Caribbean end of the Nicaraguan canal route proposed by Stephens. He claimed San Juan del Norte, well within Nicaraguan territory, and renamed it Greytown. Chatfield also surveyed the Gulf of Fonseca to establish a British claim to the Pacific entry point of any such canal. And so began a power struggle between Britain and the United States over what Pablo Neruda was to call the "delicate waist" of Central America.[8]

With competing British interests out in the open, the United States signed an agreement with New Grenada (now Colombia) for transit rights across the isthmus of Panama. Signed in 1846 and ratified in 1848, the Bidlack-Mallarino Treaty guaranteed neutrality of the isthmus, but, as U.S. President William Polk pointed out to the U.S. Senate:

The importance of this concession to the commercial and political interests of the United States cannot easily be over-rated. The route by the isthmus of Panama is the shortest between the two oceans, and from the information herewith communicated it would seem to be the most practical for a railroad or canal.[9]

Chatfield resorted again to gunboat diplomacy. The British steamship Plumper attacked and claimed Trujillo, on the Caribbean coast of Honduras, while Chatfield himself sailed for Tigre Island, a Honduran territory on the Gulf of Fonseca, occupying it in the name of the British crown.

Chatfield found a worthy U.S. adversary in Ephraim George Squier, civil engineer, archeologist, linguist, editor, railroad entrepreneur, and U.S. agent. Squier sent Chatfield an ultimatum to get off Tigre Island within six days or he would consider the invasion an act of aggression against the United States. Interestingly enough, he did not even mention the sovereign rights of Honduras over Tigre Island. The Honduran president, Juan Lindo, a Liberal, asked Squier to put Tigre Island under U.S. protection for eighteen months in order to prevent Chatfield from renewing the British claims. This marked the beginning of a history of Liberal Honduran reliance on the United States for its defence, a policy some have likened to hiring the wolf to protect the lambs.

The zeal of Squier and Chatfield embarrassed both their governments. The U.S. administration did not want a direct clash with Britain, and the British government soon discovered that gunboat diplomacy in Central America did not make it popular back home. So, in 1850, while the rival agents squared off, Britain and the United States signed the Clayton-Bulwer Treaty. Each promised it would not seek exclusive control over the proposed Nicaragua canal, and would not colonize or exercise dominion over any part of Central America. Instead, the two countries would guard the safety and neutrality of the canal and support any other canal or railway across the isthmus on the same principle.

Chatfield, however, had by no means finished his own work. He successfully undermined the Pact of León of 1851, by which Honduras and El Salvador were attempting to revive Central American federation. He supported the Costa Rican claim to San Juan del Norte, disputed by Nicaragua. He aroused open warfare between Guatemala and Honduras in 1850 by supporting a rebellion against Honduran president Juan Lindo. Finally, he went too far by interfering with U.S. financier Cornelius Vanderbilt's steamer and stagecoach trans-isthmus line across Nicaragua.

Vanderbilt had been wooing British financing in London for his railroad. These financial interests and the enemies of Lord Palmerston, the British prime minister, protested against Chatfield's gunboat diplomacy. Palmerston resigned and Chatfield was recalled. Chatfield's influence lingered on, with continuous interference in the Nicaraguan steamship route, and a seventh attempt, in 1852, to establish a British colony on the Honduran Bay Islands. Squier fulminated, self-righteously, against Chatfield's diplomacy: "The whole history of British relations and diplomacy here has been characterized by an effrontery and unscrupulousness almost incredible and absolutely unprecedented."[10]

Frustrated in his zeal to extend official U.S. influence in Central America, Squier turned his attention to plans for a Honduran railroad to rival the one being built in Panama in competition with Vanderbilt's Nicaragua line. In 1853 he signed a charter for the Honduras Inter-Oceanic Railway Company with President José Trinidad Cabañas, who once fought alongside Morazán and who preserved the earlier statesman's concept of liberal economic progress. The plan was for a track from Puerto Cortés on the Caribbean to Amapala on the Pacific, with both entry points to be declared free ports. Costs were estimated at less than $14 million, a comparative bargain, because convict labour would be used.

The concessions given to Squier reflected Honduran open-handedness to foreign investors. Squier got one thousand square miles of land, free. His company could expect $2 million a year in revenue, although all U.S. citizens were given the right to travel and work in Honduras without paying taxes or duties and without passports. In return, Honduras would get one dollar for each adult passenger carried, and a $400,000 development loan (which Honduras promptly spent on arms to fight off the Guatemalan attack encouraged by British interests).

But Squier's company failed to get sufficient financing. There were few European investors ready to risk their money in an unknown and reputedly violent land and, for the moment, plans for a railroad came to naught.

William Walker: man of destiny

Vanderbilt's control over both the Panama and Nicaraguan railroad companies was being challenged by two other prominent financiers, Cornelius Garrison and Charles Morgan. Their backing sustained the ambitions of William Walker, the "grey-eyed man of destiny" who was to proclaim himself president of Nicaragua. To the U.S. press, Walker was either a hero or a crazy adventurer. In reality, he was more of a front man for the U.S. financial interests that exerted strong influence over U.S. foreign policy.

Walker himself seemed an unlikely military adventurer. He came from a Tennessee fundamentalist family, and had tried medicine, law, and journalism as careers, with little success. Finally he tried his hand at the mercenary activity that then went by the name of filibustering.

His friend, Byron Cole, had been offered land grants in Nicaragua by its Liberal Party, in return for help in ousting the ruling Conservative Party. Cole brought in both Walker and Cornelius Garrison to fund the enterprise, and Walker and fifty-seven other Americans landed in Realejo on the Nicaraguan Pacific coast in June 1855. They found themselves facing not just a Nicaraguan army but Hondurans too, led by General Santos Guardiola. It was then that Guardiola acquired his nickname "the butcher", from his fierce resistance to Walker's army. But by October, Walker had taken Granada, and by the following June he had elected himself President of Nicaragua. He was only thirty-two years old.

The U.S. government hesitated before recognizing Walker's government. Finally, the power of the Morgan and Garrison Trust, which sent Walker arms, money, and mercenaries, prevailed against any qualms of legitimacy. Pressure also came from southern voters, who saw Nicaragua as a possible place to set up the old plantation way of life threatened by the approaching Civil War. Liberal senators agreed with Walker that Central America could profit by a dose of republicanism and U.S. enterprise, while the southerners noted Walker's willingness to allow slavery in his new Nicaragua.

There were pro-Walker rallies throughout the Southern United States. Walker supporters accused President Franklin Pierce of catering to British interests by delaying U.S. recognition. Typical of the more rabid U.S. statesmen to justify Walker's expedition was Samuel S. Cox, representative for Ohio:

Whether the races of this continent be in a tribal condition, as our Indians, or in a semi-civilized and anarchical condition, as are the Central and South American and Mexican races, they must obey this law of political gravitation. The law drives them to the greater and more illustrious State for protection, happiness and advancement. Whether the United States go and take them, or they come and ask to be taken, no matter. They must whirl in, throw off their nebulous and uncertain form, and become crystalized into the higher forms of civilization.[11]

Walker was no more tactful than Samuel Cox. He declared English the official language of Nicaragua, a move that united all the other Central American states against him. Led by Costa Rica and armed by rival U.S. financier Cornelius Vanderbilt, the Central American forces finally defeated Walker's contingent on May 1, 1857. Walker himself surrendered to a U.S. warship thoughtfully sent to take off his remaining band of two hundred soldiers. The warship's commander gave total credit to U.S. enterprise:

Vanderbilt's man had succeeded in doing what the allied Central American states could not accomplish. It was American capitalists who set up the filibuster regime in Nicaragua, and it was an American capitalist who pulled it down.[12]

Walker was no sooner home in New Orleans than he began once more recruiting for another Nicaraguan venture. Twice frustrated by U.S. naval forces, he got his final chance at glory in 1860, when British settlers on the Bay Islands of Honduras, angered by London's agreement to hand the islands back, asked for his help. He landed on the islands and attacked and occupied the port of Trujillo. A regiment of British soldiers landed right behind him, captured him and turned him over to the Hondurans, who executed him on September 12, 1860.

The time for more direct adventurism was over, for Britain as well as the United States. Britain had conceded Honduran sovereignty over the Bay Islands by the Wyke-Cruz Treaty of 1859, and recognized Nicaraguan sovereignty over the Mosquito coast by the Treaty of Managua the following year. The United States had been embarrassed by the Walker episode. It soon became embroiled in its own Civil War, while the immediate need for an inter-oceanic route diminished with completion of its own Union Pacific Railroad in 1869.

The Walker episode left a permanent scar on the U.S. image in Central America and was a factor in the decision, finally, to grant a contract for a canal to the French builder of the Suez Canal, Ferdinand de Lesseps. It was another thirty years before the United States was able to buy the Panama Canal property from France and establish its control.

The united effort to defeat Walker produced new efforts at a Central American federation. In 1871, President José María Medina of Honduras proposed an act of union that was signed by all the states except Nicaragua. But within two months of the signing, the movement disintegrated with an outbreak of skirmishing between Honduras and El Salvador.

In 1874, the U.S. ambassador to Guatemala summed up, in a dispatch, what he considered the main obstacles to union: the debts of the previous federation, local prejudices, a heterogeneous population, lack of a common interest, difficulty of inter-communication, and lack of a prominent leader. No answers to such problems were apparent.

Justo Rufino Barrios, dictator of Guatemala from 1873 to 1885, was the next to plan Central American union, under Guatemalan leadership. In 1895, Nicaragua, El Salvador, and Honduras tried again, even deciding on a federal capital to be built where their territories intersected, at the Gulf of Fonseca. But that attempt, too, foundered. The Central American nations could not separate the concept of union from the programs of the Liberal Party, which had been so discredited by the Walker episode. Leaders who had united to throw him out were Conservatives, combining forces for a necessary job, rather than idealists with any plans for united progress.

Seven years of Liberal reform

More enlightened rule returned briefly to Honduras between 1876 and 1883, with the presidency of Marco Aurelio Soto and that of his former chief aide, Ramón Rosa. Significantly, both had been in exile in Guatemala, and came to power in Honduras largely through the influence of Guatemalan dictator Justo Rufino Barrios.

Soto's slogan was "Peace, Education and Material Prosperity".[13] A Liberal with strong opinions about the state's role in development, Soto organized a postal service, a library, and a mint. He was the first to establish a proper budgetary policy; he set up free primary schooling and codes for criminal, penal, and civil law. But when he began to attempt army reform, indignant army chiefs joined forces with the clergy, who felt threatened by Liberal reform and branded Soto an atheist. He was forced to resign.

Luis Bográn, who followed Soto, tried to continue the Liberal package of reforms, using his own slogan of "Peace, Progress and Roads", but soon faced a series of attempted coups, including the takeover of the presidential palace. Civil war erupted, and the government changed hands twenty-nine times with Liberals and Conservatives alternating in power. Almost every city in Honduras suffered attack by one force or the other: from Tegucigalpa (attacked seven times from 1890 to 1924) to El Progreso (attacked in 1931).

Some of the skirmishes were local feuds. Some were a spilling over of neighbouring conflicts, establishing a pattern of defeated leaders from other countries seeking asylum in Honduran territory in order to recuperate and re-enter the fray, frequently dragging Honduran forces along with them. There was no opportunity for social or economic development. In a country desperately poor and often at war, money acquired from loans went towards guns rather than seeds. Honduran commerce had barely reached beyond the local scale; roads, money, and consumers were few. The only manufacturing before 1900 was that of soap, shoes, and candles. Ranchers with cattle to sell usually used Guatemalan middlemen, and most landowners lived off the rent of land to tenant farmers.

Forty years after Morazán, Honduras had plunged from enlightened leadership and a semblance of unity with its neighbours into a period of political chaos that was to have a profound effect on the country's social and economic life. One visitor to Honduras, a British teacher, offered a foreigner's-eye-view in 1881. María Soltera (a pen name) rode alone by horse or mule from the Gulf of Fonseca to San Pedro Sula, almost on the Caribbean:

No sane soul travels after dark, even if the only available shelter should be filthy, and all prudent men feel safer huddled together under one roof in the company of many, rather than alone or in pairs on what might be bandit-infested territory. The too-fresh memory remains of pilfering bands and commandeering troops.[14]

Obviously, from such chaos, it must have seemed that the only way out would be help from foreign powers.

6

The Banana Empires

"In Honduras, a mule is worth more than a congressman."

SAM ZEMURRAY, United Fruit Company president

In 1876 the solution to Honduras's misfortunes seemed clear to the Liberal reformers who gained power: capital investment. The Constitution of 1880 clearly stated the duty of the state to procure that investment: "The State will do everything possible to increase the welfare and development of the country, stimulating progress in agriculture, industry and trade, attracting immigration, colonizing arid land, building railroads and highways, helping new industries and establishing lending institutions, bringing in foreign capital ... through concessions and incentives."

To some Central Americans the whole region seemed to offer unlimited opportunities for investment and development that would enrich capitalists of foresight both inside and outside. Sixty years later, the Honduras poet and revolutionary Froylán Turcios looked back wryly on the aspirations of the time:

We wanted to see Central America flourishing magically among the powerful nations of the world. We wanted to see her marching with confidence towards some glorious destiny. We dreamed of seeing the countryside, from one end to the other, crossed by railroad lines in every direction, filled with the noise of engines, crowned with smoke like great war horses that galloped unceasingly, sowing progress and riches in their wake. We yearned to see her powerful and fruitful, her broad lands mounded high with crops and her rivers of gold and mountains of silver enriching her people; we heard everywhere the noise of machines and the hymn of work; we saw her cities multiplying, resplendent with iron and marble palaces. We wanted her ports to be like forests of masts, flying the flags of every country and every trading house.[1]

To the Honduran elite, after plans for a Honduran-based inter-oceanic canal had been abandoned, the new path to progress appeared to be railroads. Undeterred by George Squier's earlier failure to finance a line across the country, the Honduran government borrowed $6 million from British financiers between 1867 and 1870 to finance an inter-oceanic track that in the end was never completed or put to use. The company constructing the line collapsed and so did the only bridge along the fifty-seven miles of track from the coast. Instead of encouraging progress, this railroad venture turned into a millstone of debt. Without sufficient resources to pay even the interest, the government let the debt slide until, by 1916, that original $6 million had grown to $125 million, and the government was forced to call in U.S. financiers to renegotiate payments.[2]

There was not much to hope for from local capital. The Honduran oligarchy was rich only in land, and lacked the necessary capital to develop an export crop. The oligarchy also proved to be unskilled in management of the type of capitalist agro-production envisioned by Marco Aurelio Soto when he became president in 1876. Honduras had profited little from exports like indigo and sarsaparilla. Its more promising cattle industry had been ruined by civil disturbances and foreign invasions. A poor transportation network, a shortage of labour, and a lack of experience in foreign marketing hampered the national capacity for export development.

In the 1870s, it has been argued, Honduras was not even yet a nation, but still in a semi-feudal state.[3] Its scattered peoples had no common history except that of territorial disintegration and isolation. There was only limited internal trade and a little external trade, and no great sense of national purpose. There seemed no way that such a state could make the leap into the modern world of commerce without foreign assistance.

Still smarting from Chatfield's imperialist designs on Honduran territory, and unhappy with the British financing of what became a defunct railroad, Honduran leaders again looked to the United States for help. The Liberal leaders were admirers of the U.S. spirit of liberty and free enterprise; they saw no danger in making generous concessions to U.S. investors. And so they began by seeking U.S. investment for the nation's traditional form of production – mining.

The mineral solution

The Liberal government began, significantly enough, with a mine owned jointly by the president and his cousin – the Rosario Mine at San Juancito, twenty-five miles from Tegucigalpa. In 1880, President Soto contacted New York financiers, and together they formed the New York and Honduras Mining company, with $1.5 million in capital and complete exemption from Honduran duties or taxes. According to the agreement, Rosario Mining was to extract and export silver and gold, incidentally paying its miners infinitesimal wages and the Honduran state not one cent. The government would provide road access. Not surprisingly, President Soto kept these terms secret for seventeen years.

This was only the start. Between 1862 and 1915 various Honduran administrations granted concessions to 276 mining companies, most of them foreign owned. The aim of this multitude of grants was to spread around mining development, but by 1900 Rosario Mining had taken over most of the competitors and controlled 87 per cent of mining exports, and therefore nearly 45 per cent of all Honduran exports.[4] When the world departed from the silver standard at the turn of the century, and the bottom dropped out of the market, almost all the u.s.-owned mines shut down. In 1900, the Honduran Minister of Public Works announced that mining was practically at a standstill. Instead of priming the pump for Honduran enterprise, the mining boom had left unemployment, ravaged hillsides, and an empty national treasury.

But the Liberal reformers had another prospect that would also involve the United States: the export of fruit. One of Soto's advisers, Alfredo Zúniga, wrote in 1878:

Knowing the tendency of the United States of America to extend its commercial relations with other countries, and it being widely known that the fertile terrains of the Atlantic Coast and the Bay Islands are fit for the cultivation of tropical fruit, and that there is an extraordinary demand for these fruits in the United States at the present moment in which that great nation seeks to dominate and replace England, France and Germany in trade with us, is it right to hold any doubts that the United States is great enough to ensure our future?[5]

Soto's successor, Luis Bográn, who had held power off and on in the 1880s, had also favoured export agriculture, but was more realistic about investment payoffs: "For foreign capital to come and set up residence in this desert of a country, uncivilized and anarchical, it must be cajoled with the hopes of fat profits."[6]

It was certainly impossible for Honduras itself to market bananas. Only the United States had the steamships necessary to get the fruit to market before it spoiled. Only the United States had the capital and the marketing expertise. The United States also had the markets. It would inevitably get the "fat profits".

The banana solution

The history of the banana goes back to the fourth century B.C., when Alexander the Great discovered it in India. In 1516, a Spanish priest brought bananas to the Caribbean, where they were grown purely for local consumption until 1870. That year Lorenzo D. Baker, captain of The Telegraph, called in at Kingston, Jamaica, on his way back to Boston and bought some green bananas in the market.

Baker paid twenty-five cents a stem, each stem weighing about fifty pounds. He sold the bananas in Boston at a 1,000 per cent profit.[7] With ten friends he founded the Boston Fruit Company to market more of this lucrative fruit and, by 1890, the company had a fleet of boats on the Jamaica-to-Boston run.

But Boston Fruit was a trading company, not a plantation. Impetus for growing bananas came from the family of Henry Meigs, a U.S. railroad tycoon, who had left his nephew, Minor Keith, in charge of railroad construction across Costa Rica. Keith planted bananas along the right of way in order to bring in quick profits to finance his seventy-five-mile railroad track. The bananas sold so well that Keith formed the Tropical Trading and Transport Company, exporting bananas from Costa Rica to New Orleans.

Building a railroad and plantation empire in Central America was hazardous business; Keith's uncle and his three brothers all died of yellow fever in the jungle. But Keith prospered. He concentrated his resources, his capital, and his markets by uniting Boston Fruit Tropical Trading with several smaller companies, and got additional financing from the Morgan Trust to create the United Fruit Company. He also established a pattern of involvement in Central American politics by marrying the daughter of a former Costa Rican president, thereby entering local society. Before long, Minor Keith had become known as "the uncrowned king of Central America".

Honduran Liberal governments had hopes that local banana-growers would benefit by competition between the U.S. trading companies. In an 1893 decree they tried to support the development of local growers by forcing the trading companies to buy bananas on shore, do their own ferrying to the merchant vessels, and assume damage costs themselves rather than make the local growers take the risks for them. By the same decree they also put a tax of two cents on every stem of bananas exported; the money was supposed to help pay for primary education and road and port facility improvements.[8] The tax was repealed in 1912, by Manuel Bonilla, the first president placed in power by banana interests. Economists have estimated that if the tax had continued, the Honduran treasury would have benefited by nearly $121 million between

1912 and 1955, and the country's income would have increased by 50 per cent.[9]

Yet another government scheme to protect local growers from the banana companies proved unworkable. New legislation in 1897 demanded that foreign companies buy land only in alternate lots to prevent them from consolidating huge estates. But the companies had skilled lawyers and hired guns to back them up. The local growers were in no way organized to protect themselves against the companies that controlled the supply of necessary irrigation equipment and pesticides and the marketing of their crop, for there was no alternative internal market. Farmers who did not "co-operate" by selling their land to the big companies found their produce rejected at the wharfside as substandard.

Ramón Amaya Amador, who worked on a United Fruit plantation, recounted the story of a local farmer in his novel *Prisión Verde* (Green Prison). The company wanting the man's land began with blandishments and patriotic advice:

"See here," said the lawyer, "when you sell your property to the Company, not only will you benefit, personally, but you will also make a patriotic contribution to the progress of our country. Look how much prosperity the Company is bringing to this valley. We must collaborate with it, out of patriotism."[10]

When the farmer eventually succumbed to pressure, he was offered a mere $2,000 instead of the original $40,000 for his land. The company lawyer was praised for carrying out the eviction process much more efficiently and cheaply than if force had been used.

Along these lines, the banana empires were able to take over the fragile, local agricultural sector, making enormous profits on small investments. Cuyamel Fruit, for example, began with a $5-million investment in 1911 and sold out to United Fruit eight years later for $29 million, making a profit of 480 per cent.[11]

Much can be said for the banana companies. They took over swamp land, drained it, hired thousands of workers, brought in roads, schools, and medical clinics. It is doubtful that local farmers, without technical help, could have done such an efficient job. But the companies also brought with them all the ills of capitalist exploitation.

To thousands of peasants who had scarcely seen paper money before, the wages offered (from $24 to $55 a month in the 1920s) seemed a fortune. As a result, peasants came flocking to the coast to find work. But drinking, gambling, and high prices at the company store quickly turned the anticipated paradise into a debtors' prison as workers found themselves entirely dependent upon the company. Although there would eventually be rows of neat, modern bungalows, workers in the early days lived in overcrowded barracks, ate poorly, and suffered from recurrent bouts of malaria. Working conditions were so bad that the average useful life of a plantation worker was a mere twelve years.[12]

The crippling effect of the banana companies on economic development was just as apparent. On a local level, the company store put many neighbourhood merchants out of business. On a national level, diversification by the banana companies into banking, fishing, industry, and commerce created a new economic order that operated entirely outside of the traditional market system. The beginnings of Honduran commerce were absorbed or out-sold by the new subsidiaries, or by the European or Middle-Eastern immigrant merchants attracted to them. (By 1930, more than half the businesses in Tegucigalpa were controlled by recent immigrants.)[13]

To Hondurans living on the coast, Tegucigalpa, with its traditional bureaucracy, might have been another world. English was the language of authority. Company lawyers became powerbrokers in Honduran affairs, and the banana companies decided the outcome of Honduran political battles.

Banana wars

In the early days, competition between banana companies engendered primitive hostilities. Running battles between plantations were sometimes exploited by one company or another as a means of extending landholdings. As the bigger companies swallowed their competitors, the rivalry became more sophisticated and more injurious to Honduran society.

The first company to arrive, in 1904, was Vacarro Brothers, later to become Standard Fruit & Steamship, then Standard Fruit, and eventually a subsidiary of Castle & Cooke. It soon built fifty-five miles of rail line from its headquarters and port at La Ceiba, through its plantations on the eastern end of the banana belt, and had four boats delivering its products to New Orleans. Early diversifications brought Vacarro into every aspect of the Honduran economy: sugar, soap, oil, margarine, with a shoe factory, brewery, distillery. It even owned a bank, later to be known as Banco Atlantida, which became one of the country's two largest banks (and is now controlled by Chase Manhattan).

The Cuyamel Company came next. Set up by Samuel Zemurray in 1911 on a railroad concession owned by the German Streich company, it lay to the west of Vacarro Brothers, along the banks of the Cuyamel River and close to the port of Tela. Cuyamel's irrigation methods and efficiency soon gave it the lead in sales.

In 1929 Zemurray sold out to United Fruit, originally purely a trading company, which began operating plantations in Honduras through its subsidiaries, Tela Railroad and Trujillo Railroad, on the far east and far west of the banana coast.

"Mamita Yunai", as the local people called it, soon grew into a giant conglomerate that controlled more than one million acres of Central America as well as a fleet of a hundred vessels and most of Central America's rail lines. By 1930, it had assets of over $242 million and owned more than three million acres. By 1952 it was exporting 1.6 million stems of bananas a year, accounting for between 80 and 90 per cent of all banana trade with the United States.

Mamita Yunai was everywhere. In Cuba, Fidel Castro worked on a United Fruit plantation to pay his law-school fees. Ironically, it was the triumph of Fidel Castro's Cuban revolution and the threat of nationalization in other countries, following Cuba's example, that led United to sell most of its land-holdings in Central America and to diversify and merge until it became United Brands in 1970. Its Chiquita Bananas are still the best-known brand.

A comparison between Honduran government and company balance sheets indicates the power of the giant empires. In 1981, the whole of the Honduran export trade amounted to only 20 per cent of United Brands' total world-wide sales. Put together, the annual world sales of United Brands, Castle & Cooke, and the third conglomerate in the area, R.J. Reynolds Tobacco Company, are three times as large as the combined exports of the seven countries of Central America.[14]

Sam the banana man

One way to understand the impact of the banana companies on Honduras is to follow the story of Sam "the banana man" Zemurray, who immigrated to the United States from Bessarabia as a child. While working for his aunt and uncle in an Alabama country store, he met his first banana salesman and promptly headed for the port of Mobile, where he arranged to buy the ripe fruit rejected by regular importers. Delivering it himself overnight, he went on to build up a small wholesale business. In 1905 he sailed for Honduras to buy an old railroad concession and start his own banana company, Cuyamel.

Sam Zemurray was a new-style boss; he lived full-time in the tropics and worked constantly. His innovative use of irrigation yielded bigger and better bananas. But Zemurray was still an outsider in the big league.

United Fruit was already on close terms with the Honduran government; United fixed U.S. loans for the government, and the government gave United a virtual marketing monopoly. Zemurray needed somehow to gain his own lot of concessions, and his solution would be typically audacious: a coup d'état to depose Honduran Liberal president Miguel Dávila, who was already facing the threat of a revolution for "selling the country out to foreigners".[15]

Zemurray sought out former president Manuel Bonilla in New Orleans, where he was plotting a return to office. Zemurray bought him a surplus U.S. navy ship, the Hornet, and recruited a boatload of mercenaries, led by General Lee Christmas, a former railroad engineer with a habit of biting pieces from the rim of his glass to prove he was tough. The Hornet eluded the U.S. coastguard, sailed for Honduras with Bonilla, Zemurray, Christmas and a machine gun, and landed without opposition at Trujillo in January 1911. Shortly afterwards Bonilla also took La Ceiba. The U.S. State Department vacillated in its support for the legitimate government of President Dávila and instead worked to protect the opposition forces. With both the U.S. government and the fruit company ranged against him, Dávila resigned in March, ending the war. He was replaced by Francisco Bertrand, a candidate proposed by the "revolutionists".[16] A year later the fruit company's man, Manuel Bonilla, became president. Zemurray received vast land concessions, and General Lee Christmas got not only a brace of pearl-handled pistols but also command of the Honduran army. His lieutenant, former New Orleans policeman Guy "Machine-Gun" Maloney, was put in charge of dispossessing unco-operative peasants whose land was needed to make good the concessions granted to the Cuyamel Fruit Company. United Fruit reacted with characteristic composure, avoiding obvious opposition to the new government and thereby receiving its own share of land concessions in the northern Sula valley.

Although both Cuyamel and United Fruit were alike in defrauding the Honduran authorities by operating illegal private railroads and claiming concession land alongside "ghost" lines that were never built, they were fiercely competitive over territory. This feud became dangerous to Honduran sovereignty when the companies' lands overlapped Honduran-Guatemalan borders. Their holdings met on a poorly defined border, involving Honduras and Guatemala in a dispute that was finally settled by U.S. mediation years after both banana companies had become one in 1929. Similarly, Cuyamel's holdings in Nicaragua caused Zemurray to back Nicaragua in a boundary dispute with Honduras that almost precipitated a regional war.[17]

Within Honduras, too, politics pivoted on the fruit companies. United was a solid backer of Tiburcio Carías Andino, who crowned years of political infighting with sixteen years as Honduran dictator for the National Party, from 1932 to 1948. Zemurray and Cuyamel, on the other hand, supported any group that opposed Carías. Much more flexible than United Fruit, Cuyamel would support Liberals or anti-Carías Nationalists – in fact, anybody who opposed United Fruit. But Zemurray's bribes and influence could not match the power of United Fruit. In 1929 he decided to sell out to United in return for 300,000 United Fruit shares valued at $32 million.

Zemurray got out just before the Depression; United Fruit's profits plunged from a high of $44.6 million in 1920 to $6.2 million in 1932. Zemurray's shares plunged as well and he was furious at his own loss of a comfortable fortune. He descended on a board of directors' meeting in 1933, declaring, "You people have screwed up the company long enough." He left the meeting as United Fruit president.[18]

Until he retired in 1950 at the age of seventy, Zemurray ruled an empire that employed 82,000 workers from Colombia to Cuba. Over the years, his strategy changed from blatant manipulation to a more sophisticated public relations approach. In 1920, when he was still at Cuyamel, a letter from his vice-president H.V. Rolston to Luis Melara, the company lawyer, indicates the early style. Doubts have been raised about the authenticity of this letter, but no historian has argued against it being an accurate portrayal of common business practice. Rolston's list of instructions reads:

1 So that our great sacrifices and enormous investments will not have been made in vain, we must acquire and control as much national and private land as we can afford and absorb.

2 Our aim must be the enrichment of our company, and we must keep open every opportunity for new exploitation. In short, we must acquire as much land as our strategic interest requires, in order to guarantee our future growth and development and increase our economic power.

3 We must make our contract so tight that nobody can compete with us, not even in the distant future. Any business that becomes established must be under our control and adapt itself to our established principles.

4 We must obtain concessions, privileges, franchises, exemption from obligations which might restrict our profits and those of our associates. We must put ourselves in a privileged position in order to impose our commercial philosophy and defend our economic interests.

5 It is necessary to cultivate the imagination of our local vassals and get them to accept the idea that we are going to get rich, and to do the same with politicians and the leaders we intend to use. Observation and careful study shows us that a people degraded by alcohol are easy to assimilate to our destiny and use. It is in our interest to take care that the privileged class bows to our will, because we need them for our exclusive benefit. Generally, men such as these have no principles, strength of character or patriotism; they yearn only for position and reward, which lead them on to further appetite.

6 These men must not be allowed to act on their own initiative, but only in set circumstances under our immediate control.

7 We must break with friends who have been in our service but who we consider to have been weakened by loyalty to us; sooner or later they will betray us. We must distance ourselves without making them offended and treat them with deference even though we no longer use them. It is their country, their natural resources, their coast, their people that we still need. Little by little we shall acquire them.

8 In general, all discussion and planning must turn on these words: power, wealth, work, discipline and method. We must proceed with subtlety, not risking to espouse principles or justify our claims to power. No acts of charity, no claims to notice, in short, nothing that might reveal our real intentions. If our projects end badly, we will develop a new strategy, be more modest, more simple, more "simpático", even, perhaps, virtuous.

9 We must disrupt the growing economy of this country and increase its problems in order to favour our own aims. We must prolong its tragic, stormy life, plagued with revolution; the wind must blow only upon our sails and the waves wet only our keels.

10 We come, therefore, to the end. You know the men better than I do. When I arrive I will show you a list of the lands we must acquire, immediately where this is possible.[19]

Changing the image

From such blatant beginnings, United Fruit's machinations changed to suit the times. United operated a network of local associates whose influence extended into every sphere of Honduran life. A strong public relations presence advertised the "good will" and generosity of the company. There was even a United Fruit newspaper, the *Diario Comercial,* and a Middle America Information Office to feed the international press. In 1954, when United Fruit was at the heart of the anti-Communist hysteria against the Arbenz government in Guatemala, United Fruit paid half a million dollars a year to lobbyists and publicists in Washington in order to protect its Guatemalan holdings.[20] The subsequent CIA-organized overthrow of Jacobo Arbenz was aimed not only at protecting the Americas from "communism" but also at saving United Fruit from expropriation.

Internal operations also moved with the times. Earlier on, when the Panama fungus hit the coast in the late 1920s, the banana companies moved some of their operations to a less humid climate where bananas could better resist the plague. United Fruit abandoned its entire Trujillo division, ripping up seventy-eight miles of track and shipping it south, rails and all.[21]

Other companies sold off land to local farmers under the "associate producer" system by which the company offered seeds, fertilizers, chemicals, and packaging material and paid a certain percentage of the sale price in advance. The local farmers were left with the risk of hurricanes, flood, disease, and market fluctuations. When Hurricane Fifi hit in 1974, the big companies were protected; the associate producers suffered. This system was also a way to avoid labour troubles. Workers who went on strike against the big companies in 1954 because of low wages and poor living conditions found themselves even worse off when they were fired and had to work for smaller plantation owners who were too poor themselves to provide health care and decent wages.

As the banana companies set up more plantations on the Pacific shores of Ecuador, Panama, and Costa Rica, the Honduran banana-coast economy began to decline. Productivity programs and mechanization accelerated unemployment. By 1959, Standard Fruit and United Fruit had only half of their 1954 workforce.[22]

The legacy of foreign investment

It became obvious in 1975 that the banana companies had not fundamentally changed their ways when Eli Black, president of United Brands, mysteriously plunged to death from the forty-fourth floor of his New York office. At the time he was being investigated by the U.S. government in connection with a bribe designed to prevent the imposition of a banana export tax.

This tax of one dollar for every forty-pound box of bananas was being urged on its members by the newly formed Union of Banana Exporting Countries (UPEB). In Honduras, Standard Fruit reacted by threatening to destroy thousands of cases of bananas. United Brands evidently tried a bribe instead. A U.S. federal investigation later revealed that Black had authorized a $1.25 million bribe to Abraham Bennaton Ramos, Honduran economic minister, in the hope of saving his company some $7 million in export taxes. The "Bananagate" scandal forced President Oswaldo López Arellano to resign. But the fruit companies still won in the end. The new president, General Juan Alberto Melgar Castro of the National Party, dropped any claim to the one dollar a box tax and, to prevent future misunderstandings, recruited contacts from both fruit companies to positions of government power.

In any case, by the 1980s United Brands had moved to La Lima and diversified into palm oil and plastics. Despite this, in 1986 its Tela Railroad division in Honduras was still top banana exporter, with twenty-nine million boxes shipped out of the country. Castle & Cooke's Standard Fruit division became more of a marketing than a banana-producing company (thereby cutting another seven hundred jobs by 1982). In spite of increased productivity, both companies continued to plead poverty in order to get strikes settled by the government and to keep or improve their tax concessions.

Proof that the banana business is still a money-maker lies in continued high profits and in the arrival, in 1984, of the R.J. Reynold's subsidiary Del Monte, whose president Alfred Eames once told shareholders, "bananas are like money trees."[23] Indeed, at R.J. Reynolds, bananas account for 17 per cent of profits, though only 7 per cent of sales. Out of all sales, the banana-exporting country gets a mere 14 per cent in wages and taxes, and that small share is continually shrinking.[24] What is growing is the companies' hold over the Honduran economy, as they diversify. Today, U.S. transnational corporations not only have absolute control over the five largest firms in Honduras, they also control 88 per cent of the twenty largest and 82 per cent of the fifty largest companies.[25]

It was perhaps a fitting irony that Rosario Mining, the company that began the promise of a Honduran economic boom one hundred years earlier, pulled out in 1987, leaving 1,150 workers unemployed and a town of 24,000 people destitute. The government announced it would reduce both taxes and the mine's electrical bill for any foreign buyer ready to take over.

In the end foreign investment left a wake of rusting machinery, unemployment lines, and far-reaching social and economic effects. Historian Ralph Lee Woodward Jr., sums up the effect:

The closer relations with foreigners completed the Liberal Revolution and destroyed vestiges of Hispanic feudalism and colonialism. But it established an oligarchy of foreign domination, leaving the majority of the population to face many of the same problems they had suffered before.... Foreign companies justified unscrupulous business practices in crass Darwinian terms of survival of the fittest long after it would have been impossible for them to use such arguments at home.[26]

As Woodward concludes, the foreign companies did contribute a "certain kind of development". In Honduras the benefits of this development went mostly to foreigners, and the huge losses were left to be covered by the bulk of the local population.

7

Party Politics

" 'Banana presidents' are a product of pre-existing objective conditions and not
an incurable evil peculiar to wayward Latin Americans."
GREGORIO SELSER, author of *Honduras: República Alquilada*

Honduran political history through the late nineteenth and early twentieth
centuries is such a welter of confusion that it is tempting to avoid analysis and
present, instead, a satiric panorama of tinpot generals playing musical chairs.
Between 1824 and 1933, 117 different presidents took office, lasting an average of less than a year each. In 1876 alone, Honduras suffered through eight
presidents. One politician, José María Medina, gained and lost the presidency
eight times between 1860 and 1880.[1]

Buried under this history of near chaos, however, was the beginning of a
two-party political system. Both parties always lacked coherence and
definition; they have not represented the interests of most of the population
and have tended to freeze out other parties that might have done so. However,
the two-party system provided at least some small measure of stability as Honduras struggled to emerge from its long history of instability.

Following the failure of Morazán, and apart from two brief periods of Liberal reform under Presidents Soto and Bográn, Honduran politics descended
to the level of government by *caudillo*. This was the figure mythologized by
Latin American writers as a vulture, hyena, bison, jackal, or even, by Rubén
Darío, as a "beribboned panther". However, government by a local strong-
man was no local phenomenon fired by Latin blood, but a symptom of world
history that would be repeated, later, in other parts of the Third World during
the forced transition from semi-feudalism to capitalism. *Caudillo* rule
occurred because traditional authority broke down and insufficient ground
had been laid down for the possibilities of more democratic government. In

Honduras, the difficulty of this transition was accentuated by three centuries of static Spanish colonialism and by the precipitate and superficial nature of the Liberal reforms that followed.

Some historians ascribe the chaos in Honduras to its failure to adapt to modern times. However, it is notable that political and social chaos accompanied the rise in foreign investment. Instability was, indeed, frequently linked to the jockeying for power of the banana empires that were supposed to bring progess and riches. The seeming lack of Western-style progress may have had its own benefits. For example, the continuance of the traditional system of land claims, the *ejidos*, preserved land for the peasants and later allowed a relatively successful program of agrarian reform, compared to El Salvador or Guatemala where land had been forcibly taken away from peasants in the nineteenth century. Lack of progress may not have been all bad.

Strangely enough, the nature and effect of *caudillo* rule are also debatable – although the tendency has been to consider such a form of government as tyranny and all elected governments as benign.

Government by "caudillo"

The standard characterization of the *caudillo* is entirely negative. *Caudillo* rulers have generally been pictured as practitioners of the hero cult, as ruthless, vain, and authoritarian, as passionate, paranoid (though uncultured) demagogues who take possession of the people and then denounce personal enemies as enemies of the country. They will, so it is said, do whatever is necessary to retain power, "and more besides".[2]

But José Carlos Mariátegui and Juan Bautista Alberdi, eminent Latin American political thinkers, defended the *caudillos* as genuine folk leaders, respected keepers of the people's traditions, defenders of their way of life, even the personification of democracy. They were, Alberdi argued, "the product of their people, their most spontaneous and genuine personification".[3]

Although the Liberal elite professed to despise the *caudillo*, it often also used him:

Imbued with European political ideas, inheritors of the Enlightenment, the elites scoffed at the concepts represented by the folk *caudillo*: "barbarian" was the epithet they hurled. Yet their practice embraced a mixture of both their own *caudillismo* and liberal democracy, with inclination toward the former. They, too, felt most comfortable, certainly more secure, with a *caudillo*, albeit one who represented their own values and protected their own interests.[4]

Certainly, the *caudillo* and the later, institutionalized, military leader were both highly serviceable to foreign economic interests, since both owed no responsibility to voters and were not squeamish about bribes or burdened by principles. The vulnerability of Honduran politicians must have been tempting to U.S. politicians out to save the world for democracy and for U.S. enterprise. So Philander C. Knox, U.S. Secretary of State in 1911, justified the takeover of Honduran customs in return for a U.S. loan by quoting a conveniently unnamed "former Honduran president" who begged:

Will you not use your strong arm to give us peace – peace long enough to learn that continual revolution is not a natural order of a nation's existence? There is no act of yours guaranteeing good government which I would not welcome. How can we care for yourselves, how can we rule ourselves under such conditions?[5]

The progression from rule by *caudillos* to rule by elected political party-leaders came slowly. Elected rulers, it turned out, behaved no better than *caudillos*. Elected party-leaders packed guns, bullied their followers, and ignored (or participated in) election frauds. Their loyalties remained on the local and personal level rather than the national.

It would be easy for the banana empires to influence and even "crown" political leaders because political party principles were not clearly defined in Honduras. To understand their weakness it is necessary, first, to see what the terms "Liberal" and "Conservative" meant in Central America at the turn of the century. Conservatives, as Ralph Lee Woodward Jr. explains, were interested in maintaining the traditional two-class society, in preserving the traditional dominant roles of the aristocratic landholding elite.[6] But they also, in "noblesse oblige fashion", offered peasants a degree of protection, especially against the threatening efforts of Liberal reformers to modernize. The Conservatives "emphasized traditional Hispanic values and institutions, especially the Roman Catholic Church, and rewarded loyal Indian and *mestizo* peasants with paternalism and respect for their communal lands". Conservatives were also on the side of states' rights and against the push towards national unity. They were "xenophobic towards foreigners who threatened the traditional society with Protestantism, democracy and modernization".

The Liberals, on the other hand, tended to be in favour of economic and political modernization based on a Western European and U.S. model. They "rejected traditional Hispanic values and institutions, especially the Church, and espoused classical economic liberalism, opposing monopolies while encouraging private foreign trade, immigration and investment".

However, few Honduran politicians, Liberal or Conservative, proposed such a cogent platform. The Liberal Party was founded in 1891, with classic principles but no proposals to solve national ills. The National Party originated in the same year in preliminary discussions over a suitable name, but its early programs were more anti-Liberal than classic Conservatism, and its principles were not defined until 1927.

Some historians argue that Honduran political parties have never represented political ideas.[7] Instead, the parties have simply urged voters to vote "red" (Liberal) or "blue" (National). Similarly, the names by which supporters were known descended to mere cat-calls – *cachurecos* (cripples), *serviles* (slaves), *fiebres* (hot-heads), and *timbucos* (fatties) – or identification with a political leader (*rodistas, suazocordovistas*).[8]

When parties made common cause with Liberals or Conservatives in neighbouring republics, where the terms had more legitimate meaning, they frequently embroiled Honduras in disputes that had no real, local relevance, allowing the use of Honduran territory for other nations' political differences.

Both Liberal and National politicians resorted to the ancient practice of the *caudillos*, parcelling out the spoils of power in patronage, and either ignoring their opponents or chasing them out to some neighbouring territory, where the foes would plot their return to set the game in motion once again. Hence, there was no reconciliation with other views or interests, but a see-saw of power.

Gaining political power was not a very sophisticated process in the nineteenth century, when "Honduran-style elections" became a byword for corruption. Few Hondurans had the vote, anyway, since an eligible voter had to be male, twenty-one, and literate. In 1870, when only 10,000 out of a total population of 350,000 attended school, and when primary education had only just begun, the eligible voters probably numbered less than 25,000.[9]

Even as late as the presidential elections of 1923, bullets were as common as ballots. In that campaign, three people were killed and eighteen were wounded in Tegucigalpa. In the Department of Yoro, the military kept opposition voters away from the polls at bayonet point, and in Puerto Cortés, the sub-director of police beat off his political opponents with a pistol, accidentally wounding one of his own policemen.[10]

By the 1980s Honduran political parties still represented regions and loyalties as much as political concepts. The landowners supported the National Party; the storekeepers, small manufacturers, teachers, office workers, and sales people backed the Liberals. A map of voting patterns in three recent presidential elections indicated that the heaviest National Party support came from outlying, sparsely-populated departments like Gracias a Dios, Intibuca,

Lempira, and Copán, while most Liberal support came from the industrial centre and the banana coast.

Both parties represented the interests of the upper and middle class, although the dropping of literacy requirements in the mid-twentieth century made peasants and workers eligible to vote. The bulk of the population, then, tended to vote for whichever leader made the most noise or offered the most benefits locally. Patronage prevailed. A member of Congress was seen as somebody who would bring in a road or a school or find jobs for relatives, rather than somebody who represented a political program. Nepotism and corruption continued to plague Honduran political life, so much so that the Centro de Documentación de Honduras (CEDOH) regularly published a page of corruption news.

For example, in 1986 CEDOH revealed that $850,000 a month in salary cheques was going to 725 Tegucigalpa civic employees who never came to work, including some who sent for their pay from overseas. Another tidbit was that eleven of the nation's fifteen road tractors were stationed in La Paz, the tiny home town of former president Suazo Córdova.[11] La Paz, a town of ten thousand people, became famous when Suazo Córdova built a 35,000-seat $1.5 million soccer stadium there, although it has no soccer team.[12] Such "advantages" were small potatoes compared with scandals in state enterprises, like the State Investment Corporation (CONADI), which lost nearly $300 million in seven years through corruption and ineptitude.

Charges of corruption have always been made at election time, because it has been easier to throw stones than to put forward real political programs. The squabbles have often been sharper within, rather than between the parties, for both parties have been prey to continual divisions, due to lack of any clear party line.

Although the Liberal Party has tended to have majority support, it has governed only 31.5 per cent of the time since inception. Divisions within the party frequently opened the door to power for a National Party that was based on the landowning oligarchy but attracted other sectors with its call for law and order. National Party principles, however, have been similarly ill-defined. They were, rather, personalized in the actions and style of Tiburcio Carías Andino, the Nationalist President and virtual dictator from 1933 to 1948.

Dictatorship – Honduran style

Carías governed simultaneously with other Central American dictators – Ubico in Guatemala, Hernandez Martínez in El Salvador, Somoza in Nicaragua – but his career was characteristically Honduran. A ladino of both

Indian and black background, he served as cook, at the age of sixteen, to a band of Liberal guerrillas, and worked for that party for twenty years. He received an honorary law degree for his services, thereby acquiring the double-barrelled prefix *Doctor y General* before leaving the Liberal ranks. Tired of the slowness of promotion in that party, he switched to the National Party in 1923 and became famous in the civil skirmishes of that year as the first commander in the world to engage in aerial bombing of civilians. When he was elected as president in 1932, he put down a Liberal revolt by calling in air support from a barnstorming pilot, a man who later set up Transportes Aereos de Centro América (TACA).

Carías held on to power by force of arms and by political manoeuvring. He changed the constitution that barred re-election, and quashed or ignored the Congress. He promoted the interests of the United Fruit Company, which financed both his party and his government for years.

Carías made good copy for visiting journalists. Six feet four, weighing 260 pounds, he was eccentric, irascible, puritanical, and tyrannical. He carried a cane and wore a fedora, but his thick leather belt and cheap rough-cut boots bespoke his peasant origins.[13]

Carías was so intent on forestalling opposition that he banned baseball in case the bats could be used as weapons against him. He changed his mind only when a young nephew convinced him that pitching could be good practice for soldiers training to throw grenades. His tyranny was often embarrassingly rustic. So those who opposed him might have their cars "imprisoned" and their daughters' beaux warned off from their courting.[14]

But his dictatorship was no joke. Carías gagged the press and jammed the prisons. He created an institutionalized dictatorship that combined political, military, and economic force. He created, for example, a system of *comandantes de armas* – "commanders at arms" – who were members of the National Party and empowered to control a particular region with army support and no questions asked. Thus the National Party became identified with regional military control.

Repression was vicious, and there was no use complaining about corruption or injustice. In 1940, when Carlos Sanabria, Commander at Arms for the Department of Colón, exceeded the customary level of human rights abuse by wiping out entire villages, Carías told a delegation of local women: "Would that I had seventeen like him." His strategy against opposition quickly became known as "*encierro, destierro y entierro*" – "round them up, throw them out, and bury them". So a peaceful demonstration in San Pedro in 1944 was fired upon by troops who killed more than one hundred unarmed civilians.[15]

The most hated decree that Carías passed was the Ley Fernanda, by which hundreds of innocent people were jailed on the charge of aiding Communism. Such excesses became embarrassing to a U.S. government embarked on a "good neighbour" policy that was out of tune with more obvious dictators. By 1948 the time was ripe for elections.

Political see-saw

Elections would ostensibly produce civilian rule, but from 1948 to 1981 the military would repeatedly step in, eventually becoming an independent political force of its own. Ironically, a military ruler sometimes proved to be more enlightened than a civilian; and the least promising of the civilian presidents sometimes proved the most able. So Manuel Gálvez, the war minister hand-picked for the presidency by Carías in 1948, nevertheless released political prisoners, encouraged the return of exiles, stopped open repression of the labour movement and began to create a modern economic infrastructure.

Too far a swing to the right, like that of Nationalist Ramón Cruz in 1971, would result in public protests and bring about a military coup to put them down. Too far a swing to the left, like that of Ramón Villeda Morales (1957 to 1963), would inevitably upset the army and thereby produce yet another coup. The resulting term of military rule might be as incompetent as that of Policarpo Paz García (known irreverently as "Inca Paz" or "the incapable") in 1980, or as responsive and astute as that of Oswaldo López Arellano (1963 to 1971 and 1972 to 1975).

López's populist military government accomplished reform without totally antagonizing the right wing. For example, his agrarian reforms answered the pressure of the growing peasant movement, yet also allowed landowners to divide up their land among family members and thus avoid expropriation. López pleased the labour sector by introducing a minimum wage, and pleased the incipient business sector by encouraging industrialization. But he failed to appease the traditional wing of the military, which resented his popularity with the more progressive officers. A charge of corruption in 1975, in the wake of the United Brands bribery scandal known as Bananagate, forced his resignation and replacement with a military junta. Military rule in Honduras has, indeed, often been as vulnerable as any civilian rule, and a charge of corruption the easiest way to ease somebody out.

Inevitably, this political see-saw was a poor preparation for elections in 1981. Both major parties had failed to move much beyond the "palace and barracks" style of politics of the turn of the century, in which power was the goal, rather than the means to govern. But, if the major political parties are so unresponsive, why is it, then, that Hondurans regularly vote for them? In the

1981 elections, 80 per cent of registered voters cast their ballots, and in 1985 the figure was 89 per cent.[16] The turnout is high, it seems, because election day is a great giveaway. Elvia Alvarado, a Honduran peasant leader, says that on election day everybody votes:

The people love to vote, they stand in long lines to vote. Election day is a big holiday. But why? Because the people are so excited about the candidates? No. Because on election day the politicians kill a bunch of cows and give away lots of food, lots of meat. For many people it's one of their only chances to eat meat.[17]

While there might be four or five parties running, the Liberals and the Nationalists have the richest coffers, so they can offer voters "the best spread" and the *campesinos* often end up voting for them. According to Elvia Alvarado:

You ask poor Hondurans why they vote for the Nationalist Party and they'll say, "Oh, because my grandfather and my great-grandfather were Nationalists. I was born a Nationalist." The same with the Liberals.

So we're really the ones to blame, because we vote for these parties. We're the ones who put these corrupt politicians in power. Because most of the poor are still ignorant, and continue to vote for the traditional parties.[18]

Given that the major Honduran political parties are an avenue to power rather than a form of government, and given the intensely practical nature of the Honduran people, it is no wonder that the smaller political parties have found it hard to gain either legal status or majority support. They have been trying for both ever since the 1960s.

The Christian Democrat Party (PDCH) was formed in 1968, but was blocked from legal status for thirteen years by a Supreme Court largely controlled by the National Party. Before it gained official status in time for the 1981 presidential elections, the PDCH made a brief alliance with more left-wing groups, forming a Honduran Patriotic Front (FPH), but even coalition – a common power lever in Honduras – failed to win it votes. On gaining legal status, it left the FPH, but won only one seat in 1981 and two in 1985. Such small support can best be understood in terms of voter traditionalism.

Although the PDCH gathers few votes, it has considerable respect, most of it due to its outspoken deputy, Efraín Díaz Arrivillaga. Another reform party, the Innovation and United Party (PINU), sprang up in 1970 with a platform based on economic modernization, but its "limousine" business image failed to bring mass support; from three seats in 1981 it dropped to two in 1985.

The three left-wing parties, the Communist Party (PCH), its Maoist splinter group (PCH-ML), and the Socialist Party (PASOH) united within the Honduran Patriotic Front to contest the 1981 elections but moved later into wider coalitions with union, peasant, and human rights groups: The National Unitary Direction (DNU) in 1983, the Committee for the Defence of National Peace and Sovereignty in 1984, and the Co-ordinating Committee of Popular Organizations (CCOP), which became a major mass movement.

What happened in Congress would become less and less relevant as the return to civilian power in 1981 revealed the major parties' stagnation and impotence. Power had gathered in the hands of interest groups such as labour or business, but those who held the ultimate power – the military – would show that the man who rules in Honduras is still the man with the gun. This time, the guns would be courtesy of the United States of America.

8

The Rise of Labour

"Employees in the banana fields are the human slag of Central America and the Antilles ... they have nothing to complain about."

CARLOS IZAQUIRRE, National Party Congressman

The labour movement in Honduras developed from a combination of home-grown, mutual assistance societies and the importation of more militant workers from the Caribbean. In fact, the labour policies of foreign companies largely provided both the grounds for protest and organization and workers capable of protest.

The dynamic of that struggle between foreign companies and labour has dominated Honduras since 1950, taking over much of the fire from party politics. A union came to mean as much to a Honduran worker as any political party. Although some unions, too, have betrayed workers' interests, and although party politics have meshed with labour politics in a peculiarly Honduran manner, only within the labour and peasant movements have Hondurans been able, as yet, to organize in defence of their rights, sometimes with considerable success.

Labour as wealth

A shortage of labour has always plagued Honduras, ever since the native population was decimated in early colonial times and there weren't enough workers to operate the mines. The British railroad builders had to import Jamaican workers in 1869. Those same railway owners called out Honduran troops when the foreign labourers protested against inhuman working conditions in the only way unorganized workers could – by desertion.

The foreign rail-gangs did not have any effect upon Honduran workers, who were as yet unorganized. But by the 1920s, when Caribbean workers were brought in to the banana plantations, the melting pot of races, experience, and expectations brought the Honduran labour conflict to a boil.

There were, of course, very few wage-earning workers in Honduras before the end of the century, since the nation was a predominately rural society. A census taken between 1881 and 1887 showed that 57 per cent of workers were self-employed, whether as peasant farmers, miners, or artisans.[1] In the cities, a few artisans and tradespeople belonged to mutual societies, whose function was primarily social – to help pay for medicine or funerals, for instance. Later, these mutual societies would develop a more militant stance, but they would be following rather than leading the surge of protest that arose among the large workforce employed by foreign companies.

The Honduran labour movement became established first among miners employed by Rosario Mining Company in 1909. A series of mining accidents led to a strike for better working conditions and better pay. The San Juancito police, paid by Rosario Mining, attacked and wounded many strikers. The Liberal government of Miguel Dávila then sent military reinforcements and a "negotiating" team who together forced the miners back to work and jailed their leaders.[2]

Because foreign companies were prepared to repress worker protests, much of the labour organization had to be clandestine, and many of the ideas publicly expressed were therefore strictly utopic. It is interesting to see the mix of resolutions passed at the First Central American Congress of Workers, held in San Salvador in 1911: resolutions for the establishment of co-operatives, for an eight-hour day, for night schools, clinics, and campaigns against alcoholism, and a motion urging workers to seek election to municipal and congressional office. One Honduran proposal actually mentioned the word "Communist", but it was for creation of a "Communist colony" in the Mosquitia as a way to resolve the problems of Honduran workers.[3]

Militant ideas of labour power, however, were not publicly propounded until 1916; significantly, this was the same year as the first strike on the banana coast, at Cuyamel Fruit.

The strikes begin

On July 10, 1916, the left-wing newspaper *El Cronista* published an editorial proposal:

The working class, which works, produces, consumes and constitutes the national conscience, which spills its blood in civil strife and succumbs in defence of the

79

homeland in international battles, must convert itself into a social factor of the first order, because it represents the majority of public opinion and the positive strength of the nation.[4]

That same month, more than six hundred workers at Cuyamel struck against the practice whereby they were paid at one rate of exchange for the Honduran lempira, and charged a higher rate of exchange in the company store. When Cuyamel hired scab labour, the strikers destroyed the bananas with their machetes. Cuyamel called in the local military, which took forty workers to jail in the Omoa fortress. Surprisingly, the commander of the fort refused to take them in and freed them, saying he thought their demands perfectly just.

Strikes began to break out in other companies. In 1920, at Vaccaro Brothers (later to become Standard Fruit), more than a thousand workers took over the company offices and much of La Ceiba itself. The Liberal president, Rafael López Gutiérrez, declared a national state of siege and sent in troops, forcing the workers to return without having gained their demands.

Another strike, in 1925, began at a sugar mill in La Lima and subsequently spread to the banana workers at Cuyamel. They demanded a raise to $2 a day, weekly paydays, an eight-hour day, a 25 per cent reduction in prices at the company store, and medical attention for workers' families. They won a few of their secondary demands, but had to return to work without a major victory.[5]

Four aspects of the early strikes deserve special note:

- They took place in each of the big fruit companies and quickly spread from sector to sector;
- The more serious demands were ignored, but some secondary demands were met, indicating a desire on the part of the company to accommodate without ceding real power;
- The employers and the Honduran government alike could call on military force to repress the strikers; and
- U.S. diplomats blamed the strikes on foreign provocateurs, accusing them of stirring up anti-American sentiments.[6]

Employers and governments alike ignored the abysmal working conditions that caused the strikes. United Fruit boasted about its resplendent offices and hospital, but was generally considered cold and intransigent towards its workers. Cuyamel, under Sam Zemurray, prided itself on the human touch; Zemurry handed out Christmas presents and insisted that his company was one happy family. But few workers felt the same way. They often laboured twelve hours a day at harvest time; they had an average of one accident a year, and 31 per cent of those living in camps unscreened against mosquitoes were infected with malaria.[7]

Dr. José A. López at the United Fruit hospital in Puerto Castilla described a "paradise of sadness and disease" in 1930:

There is an air of dreaminess about [the banana workers] that verges on apathy, as they lounge in front of their camps. The insidious laziness is induced by impoverished blood, where the plasmodia of malaria have been playing havoc.... They lie in their hammocks, smoking and looking at the sky; they sit on the railroad tracks, and grunt as approaching trains disturb their repose.[8]

He does not add that exhaustion and malnutrition accompanied malaria to achieve this effect. But Ramón Amaya Amador, who worked for eight years in banana plantations, conveys the struggle these workers had to put up just in order to keep working:

The workers continued gnawing at their implacable fate. Under the banana plants, from sun up to sun down, watched over by *criollo* foremen and gringo bosses, breathing in poison, tying up stalks, weeding, watering day and night, building, driving tractors, cars, trucks, locomotives, struggling hand to hand against tropical diseases, against malnutrition, against the misery around them.... They lived tied to the plantations, as if part of them; they became lost amid the leaves and stalks, the animals and the machines. They clung to the earth in battle against nature that threatened to devour the plantations. It was a fight between human beings and vegetation, a struggle to give life to the banana plants and the fruit that produced wealth.[9]

Amaya Amador chronicled the fighting spirit of the banana workers, and the difficulties they encountered in gaining support from the workers in the city, who had been led to believe banana workers were foreign riff-raff, lawless and violent. The authorities recognized the danger they posed, and tried to separate them from the rest of the Honduran labour movement.

Federation begins

The first Honduran Workers' Federation (FOH) was organized in 1921, with very much the same mixture of demands as those voiced at the regional conference ten years earlier. Five years later, the Federation of Workers' Societies of the North was formed, along much more combative lines. Both agreed to a Workers' Constitution that satisfied some measure of their different objectives. For the first time, the unions turned their backs on the traditional Liberal and National parties, even forbidding their workers from involvement in these parties – a measure that favoured recruitment to the Honduran Communist Party, which had been operating clandestinely since 1927.[10]

Worker militancy increased with the organization of the Honduran Union Federation (FSH) in 1929. The FSH united both worker and peasant groups, attacked the less militant FOH as "traitors of proletarian freedom", and decided to concentrate its efforts on organizing workers on the banana coast. The objectives of the FSH went beyond better wages and working conditions; they included the destruction of capitalist imperialism. With the FSH as leader, strikes began among banana workers in 1929. Confrontation with banana company goons known as the White Guard only encouraged support from fellow workers in the ports. On January 3, 1932, 180 port workers of Tela Railroad, a United Fruit subsidiary, went on strike against a wage reduction. The railroad workers went out to back the strike; even the two hundred men hired as strike-breakers changed sides and refused to work.

The same month, workers struck at another United subsidiary, Trujillo Railroad. Suppression of the strike was to become typical of the new combination of methods for dealing with labour: bribery allied to force. John Turnbull, United Fruit director in Honduras, went to the strike scene along with General Salvador Cisneros of the Honduran Army. According to the U.S. vice-consul, Turnbull bribed the organizing secretary of the strike committee, got from him a secret list of leaders, and passed it on to Cisneros, who arrested and deported the men named.

The United States saw Communist inspiration in every strike. "Without Soviet funds, how else could three thousand workers maintain themselves and their families while on strike?" questioned U.S. Ambassador Julius Lay.[11] He was particularly incensed when some workers proposed Manuel Cálix Herrera, a FSH leader and a Communist, as a candidate in the presidential elections of 1932. His fears were shared by the elected president, Tiburcio Carías, who closed all labour organizations, shut down newspapers, and outlawed demonstrations. The Communists, accustomed to clandestine operations, were better able to survive than the overt labour organizations.

Although the following president, Manuel Gálvez (1949-54), officially recognized the right to strike, to organize, and to demand a minimum wage after the 1954 banana strike, complete union legalization did not come until 1959 in Honduras. Even then, repression frequently continued on the Caribbean coast.

The banana strike

The summer of 1954 was the turning point in the history of the Honduran labour movement. That year's general strike would not have been possible without the organization of solidarity groups in the cities of the interior into the

Trade Union Unity Committee (CUS). This new formation was to be an important bulwark for the strikers.

The strike, coinciding with the U.S.-inspired campaign to unseat Guatemalan president Jacobo Arbenz, gave strength to the union movement but also hastened its subversion by U.S. labour advisers. It brought a vicious backlash from which Honduran labour still has not completely recovered.

Workers grew restless when two United Fruit Company offices refused to pay double time, as stipulated by the government, for work carried out on the Sunday of Holy Week. The suspension of one stevedore for having dropped a stem of bananas (worth barely ten cents) added to workers' grievances, and a strike at Puerto Cortés began. The workers at Tela also formed a strike committee that included stevedores and hospital workers; they demanded a 50 per cent pay hike, giving United Fruit forty-eight hours to reply. When the company insisted on thirty days to consider, the Tela workers struck. Soon the strike had spread to El Progreso and La Lima, and by May 5 all those working for both United Fruit and Standard were on strike. By May 13, workers at Rosario Mining, the Honduran Brewery, and the British American Tobacco Company had joined in; the total number of strikers had reached fifty thousand.

Peasant families fed the strikers; telegraph workers cut the line to Tegucigalpa; students, teachers, and small tradesmen contributed to the strike fund. The campaign became an unprecedented show of worker solidarity. But it was broken by a new form of U.S. intervention: the undermining of Latin American union militancy by the funding of passive alternative unions. Used alongside more old-fashioned repression, this new strategy was alarmingly successful.[12] Honduras became the test case for a policy to be used throughout the Third World in order to preserve it from communism, for capitalism.

The original strike committee at United Fruit set up local support groups and was prepared for a long walk-out, but internal division began to disrupt strike unity. One leader at La Lima accused another member of the central committee of being a Communist and began to insert his own agents into other local committees. Then, on May 19, the strikers at Standard Fruit returned to work after gaining some of their demands. They found out, only too late, the consequences of accepting an agreement stipulating that economic layoffs could in no way be considered strike reprisals and were therefore legal.

At the same time the U.S. campaign against the reform government of Jacobo Arbenz in Guatemala intensified. John Foster Dulles, U.S. Secretary of State, declared in May 1954, that "The government of Guatemala is not foreign to the strike disturbances in Honduras".[13] Invasion of Guatemala from

Honduran territory followed soon after, and influenced public perception of the strike.

Four members of the central strike committee were arrested as Communists; a second strike committee therefore gained control and signed an agreement with United Fruit on July 6. The pressure to negotiate came not just from the Gálvez Nationalist government and from United Fruit, but from George Meany, AFL president. Meany had insisted to fruit company executives in 1954 that "Unless the position of those who defend the cause of democracy and liberty is reinforced, unions will fall into the hands of militant communists, which would have disagreeable consequences for our country's position in Latin America."[14]

The strikers did make some gains. Those who returned to work got a $20 reward, promise of paid vacations, and medical treatment for their families. However, the 10 to 15 per cent wage increase was nothing like the 50 per cent they had demanded. The strikers won official recognition of a United Fruit Workers' Union (SITRATERCO), a measure which opened the way for the first Honduran labour code in 1959. However, the fact that the strike settlement was signed with the second strike committee, which was both compliant and anti-communist, opened the way for Honduras to become headquarters for U.S. unionism in Latin America. SITRATERCO was to be its shining example.

ORIT and AIFLD and labour repression

U.S. union influence had begun much earlier in Honduras, but had been outlawed, along with any form of union activity, by Carías. Now, the second strike committee invited the Inter-American Regional Organization of Labour (ORIT) to Honduras. ORIT was a hemispheric labour organization formed in 1951 and maintained by the American Federation of Labour (AFL). The three ORIT officers who moved to Honduras, with the support of the U.S. Embassy, were to reorganize a labour movement more acceptable to both the United States and the banana companies.

United Fruit was happy to co-operate with the ORIT advisers. Its public relations man, Ed Whitman, agreed:

It is only a question of time before an international and anti-communist union organization controls Honduras and the rest of the region.... Our best position is to accept it with grace, but at the same time do everything possible to see that any ambitious union leaders do not become excessively strong.[15]

The U.S. Agency for International Development (AID) built SITRATERCO an office in La Lima for $45,000, and in 1955 ORIT advisers guided the creation of SITRASFRUCO, a similar union for Standard Fruit workers.[16]

Proof of the compliance of both SITRATERCO and SITRASFRUCO was their unwillingness to intervene when floods along the north-coast rivers, coincidental with an outbreak of Panama disease on the plantations, provided the fruit companies with an excuse for massive firings. In 1954, United Fruit had twenty-six thousand workers, by 1957 only thirteen thousand. Standard also fired about half its workers between 1954 and 1959, making a total of nineteen thousand workers unemployed. Those who kept their jobs found themselves having to adapt to higher productivity standards that made more money for the fruit companies but gave them no higher wages.

The more militant workers fought for independence, but the labour law of 1959 prohibited the existence of more than one trade union per company; many independent unions disappeared or were destroyed in a 1963 military coup.[17] More compliant or ambitious workers found themselves avidly courted by the ORIT organizers, as one United Fruit worker relates:

After the strike, the AFL-CIO, the U.S. Embassy and ORIT fell on us like a plague, offering us scholarships, study in Puerto Rico and all kinds of favours from our employers.... The U.S. consul overwhelmed us with visas.... Not only did the companies grant permission for us to spend months on leave, but those workers were favoured with the choicest jobs and placed as union leaders when they returned.[18]

U.S. Congressional hearings later revealed that the U.S. Central Intelligence Agency lent both financial support and guidance, through the AFL, to the formation of ORIT and its education branch, the American Institute for Free Labour Development (AIFLD). After its establishment in 1961, AIFLD became involved in a number of military coups, including Guyana and Brazil in 1964, and Chile in 1973.[19]

ORIT was nothing if not efficient. By spring 1957, Honduras had twenty-nine unions representing about forty-five thousand workers, making the largest organized labour force in Central America. Most of the unions were ORIT-inspired.[20] During the period from 1962 to 1974, AIFLD trained 15,154 Honduran workers as labour leaders at local education centres, and sent another hundred to advanced courses in Virginia. Fears of the spread of communism after the Cuban revolution made control of Latin American unions even more vital to U.S. interests. United Fruit, W.R. Grace, Shell, ITT, Exxon, and IBM were among ninety companies making donations to AIFLD.[21]

There was to be an ominous alliance between ORIT labour and the Honduran military. In fact, the ORIT unions were among the first supporters of the

1963 military coup by General Oswaldo López Arrellano. The general even wrote to the SITRATERCO leadership, announcing his pleasure that "The two new forces in the destiny of Honduras, the armed forces of the republic and free and democratic unionism, coincide in the most fundamental of their positions on the great problems of our nation".[22]

The following year, the ORIT unions formed the Confederation of Honduran Workers (CTH), including the most powerful of the banana workers' unions and the largest peasant organization, the National Association of Honduran Peasants (ANACH).

In 1965 more militant labour leaders briefly won control of another important federation, the Central Federation of Honduran Free Trade Unions (FECESITLIH). They called for a general strike to protest repression at the Río Lindo textile plant in San Pedro Sula. The strike was put down by the military. They tried again in 1968, striking against an increase in food prices caused by the Central American Common Market agreements. This time they received support from local business, but the military occupied San Pedro Sula, closed down all newspapers, jailed strike leaders, and declared a state of siege.

Attacks on the labour movement became a normal state of affairs. So Pedro Antonio Brizuela, a union organizer who learned union politics as a teenager on a United Fruit plantation in 1954, was jailed in 1965 and fired routinely in 1967. He found himself being dismissed from his job every time a union election was coming up, so he couldn't be re-elected. The manager, a Cuban exile, would withdraw his dismissal the day after the election.[23]

Thirteen years later, Rolando Vindél González, president of the Union of National Electric Company Workers (STENEE), was arrested and tortured for days with electric shocks and the hood (*capucha*). In 1984 STENEE called for a national strike to back its demand for a 10 per cent wage increase – an increase that amounted to only $400,000 for a company that made $25 million in profits that year. Rolando Vindél González was kidnapped on his way to work and never seen again. One thousand union affiliates who demonstrated against his disappearance were arrested.[24]

The professional association of Honduran teachers (COLPROSUMAH) also came under continual attack. The military occupied its offices during a 1982 teachers' strike, and tried to impose a more compliant leadership.

New labour federations

In recent decades two new labour organizations arose to challenge the CTH-ORIT camp. The Christian Democrats began to organize trade unions during the 1960s, culminating in formation of the General Congress of Workers (CGT) in 1970. Its main strength was among the workers in Tegucigalpa.

A counterpart peasant organization led to the National Union of Peasants (UNC), challenging the ORIT-inspired ANACH. In the 1980s UNC claimed seventy-five thousand members, close to ANACH's eighty-seven thousand.[25] In 1981 a third labour federation was formed: the United Federation of Honduran Workers (FUTH), affiliated internationally with the largely Communist-dominated World Union Federation.

The membership figures provided by these three federations differ vastly from those given by the Honduran government, which insists that only 142,000 of the total labour force of more than one million are members of any union. The federations' count adds up to more than double the government union figures: the CTH claims seventy-two unions and over 100,000 workers; the CGT claims seventy-eight unions and over 125,000 workers; and the FUTH claims thirty unions and 50,000 members.[26]

All three union federations are subject to continual internal divisions. The FUTH and, until recently, the CGT have also suffered government repression. Red-baiting tactics that once saw them accused of being directed by the Soviet Union or Cuba have now shifted to pointing out alleged links with the Sandinistas in Nicaragua. But the U.S.-backed contra war against Nicaragua has also united the three union federations in protest, in spite of serious differences of principle.

The National Council of Workers and Peasants of Honduras (CONOCH) encompassed all three groupings when it began in 1985, but expelled the FUTH in 1986, and now covers just the CTH and CGT groupings. There is, however, considerable cross-over. For example, the National Congress of Rural Workers, formed in 1985, has political sympathies more allied to the FUTH than to CONOCH, to which it is affiliated.

The FUTH has its own umbrella group, the Co-ordinating Committee of Popular Organizations (CCOP), formed in 1984, which includes neighbourhood groups, peace groups, students, and women's organizations. All affiliations remain fluid. There may or may not be combined May Day parades, for instance, but there is greater spirit of unity among the younger labour leaders than the old guard, who still cling to old feuds.

Political sympathies also shift with changes in power. For example, the Christian CGT has moved further towards the National Party largely because of growing unhappiness with the Liberal government's neglect of the labour and peasant movement.

United action against the government has become more possible because peasants and workers are united in bearing the brunt of economic hard times. Each year another forty-five thousand peasants move to the city, joining the ranks of the unemployed, whose numbers, in 1986, represented 41 per cent of the workforce.[27] This large pool of labour, ready to work for any wage, makes it tough for unions to fight for better wages for their workers. And in Honduras, the labour force is not highly skilled and is therefore easily replaceable. Although there is fierce competition for jobs, there is also a history of labour organization through which one sector's struggles have enriched and informed the other. This has been particularly true of the *campesinos desproletariazados*, former fruit company workers joining the struggle for land.

Despite labour repression, it is still true that no Honduran president acts without testing what the workers will say. He may defy them, placate them, bribe them, repress them, but he cannot afford to ignore them.

9

Peasants and Priests

"All we were doing was recovering what was ours to begin with."
                    MARCIAL CABALLERO, National Union of Peasants

Land hunger: These words seem a contradiction in a country as sparsely populated as Honduras. Yet the desperate need for land, for agrarian reform, is one of the country's most pressing issues. The need has fuelled a peasant movement that has become the most powerful force in Honduras. Honduran peasants are not asking for what they never had; they are demanding what once was theirs under a system of land ownership that was not seriously threatened until the beginning of the twentieth century.

In 1895, Honduras had a population of slightly less than 400,000, compared to 700,000 in El Salvador, a country one-fifth the size.[1] Much of Honduras was still common land. Many titles were held in common under the old system of the *ejido,* or Indian land title, dating back to Spanish colonial times. In neighbouring countries, most of these titles had been seized during the last part of the nineteenth century by oligarchies concentrating on export agriculture based on crops such as coffee, cotton, and sugar. But Honduran soil was poor and its population too sparse for labour-intensive plantation agriculture. Its landowners were not interested in the management and marketing of export crops, so the bulk of the land remained available for subsistence farming.

Few of the native peoples who had originally owned *ejido* titles had survived as tribes, so their land soon passed into the common domain. Father James Carney refers to the Jesuit mission among the Jicaque tribes in the Department of Yoro in 1886. Father Manuel de Jesús Subirana helped them confirm their titles, "so that these lands with their boundary marks will be handed over when all the families of the tribe live together around a school and a church, which they must build."[2] But most of the native people had long lost their identity and their lands passed on to the ladino peasants around them. So the concept of community through land ownership spread, even though other native traditions faded. As late as 1952, 52 per cent of the national territory was still either owned by the state or *ejido* land.[3]

The state had confiscated land from the church during the 1829 and 1876 Liberal reform periods. Some of this land was gradually sold off cheap, to cover government debts to the few rich landowners. Still, there was no real land shortage for the Honduran peasant until the twentieth century.

Even the arrival of the banana companies did not, at first, threaten the availability of land for subsistence farming. The banana holdings were vast. By the 1930s the banana companies owned almost a million acres of Honduran territory.[4] This was more than a tenth of the country's arable land, but most of it was too swampy to grow other crops. In Honduras there was still room, even by the 1950s, for the 85 per cent of the population who lived off the land.

After the banana strike of 1954 the fruit companies began to mechanize, dismissing half their labour force and moving into different export crops such as cotton and sugar that required use of land already being farmed by the peasants. The work dismissals created an experienced and stubborn labour movement. Many of the dismissed workers were originally peasants themselves; they would lead the new peasant movement that sought to secure land against encroachment by private enterprise. Other countries produced very separate labour movements – industrial unions and peasant organizations. In Honduras there was not the same distinction.

When United Fruit evicted some of its former workers from unoccupied land that it wanted for its cattle operations, the workers-turned-peasants used their union experience to resist, forming the Central Committee of Peasant Unity. In 1962, the reorganized committee, now the National Federation of Honduran Peasants (FENACH), had fifteen thousand members.

Members of the Honduran Communist Party were among the first organizers of the peasant union, a fact that disturbed the fruit companies, the government, and the officials of the more compliant banana unions grouped under the leadership of ORIT (Inter-Regional Organization of Labour). With ORIT assistance, in 1962 they formed the National Association of Honduran Peasants (ANACH), a peasant coalition in competition with FENACH. ANACH copied the tactics used to win over dissident labour unions – harassment and bribes – until the peasant movement seemed well under ORIT control.

But another peasant organization was also forming. The Honduran Catholic Church had begun rural education in 1961, with a string of radio schools, and in 1964 the Social-Christian Peasant Association (ACASCH) was founded, based on a network of church community groups. Five years later it became the National Union of Peasants (UNC), a member of the General Congress of Workers (CGT) with affiliation to the Latin American Confederation of Workers (CLAT) and the World Confederation of Labour (WCL). The UNC proved to be a powerful alternative to ANACH, which shared the anti-communist stance of its ORIT counterpart, the Honduran Confederation of Workers (CTH).

The peasant organizations were the real engine for agrarian reform in Honduras. As one peasant leader expressed it: "The government gives away nothing. In Honduras, we are the agrarian reform."[5]

U.S. fear of communism following the Cuban Revolution turned out to be another motivating force for agrarian reform. The Kennedy administration pressed for social and especially agrarian reform as an alternative to revolution, tying its aid to compliance with its suggestions for reform. Ramón Villeda Morales, the reformist Liberal president from 1957 to 1963, found his own concept of reform dovetailing neatly with that of Kennedy's Alliance for Progress, since both included respect for property and opposition to communism. However, the fruit companies and landed oligarchy were not so understanding of the need for cautious reform. In order to keep the peace Villeda had to try to appease them with land concessions and offer them credit for their export crops (coffee, beef, and cotton) while at the same time satisfying the peasants' hunger for land.

The pressure for land came from all sides at once. Large landowners, seeking post-war profits in cattle-raising and cotton, needed more land. Between 1952 and 1965, the number of cattle raised in Honduras rose from 431,000 to 719,000, while cotton plantations increased in size from 12,000 acres in 1950 to 45,000 acres in 1965.[6] Many landowners evicted their tenants and some simply put up barbed-wire fences on public land.[7] Evicted peasants looking for land to rent had to compete with workers dismissed by the fruit companies and with Salvadoran migrants who had been dispossessed in their homeland. Honduran peasants saw their entitlement to public land as a legal right, and their land invasions as legal recuperation. As they organized to protect their interests, so too did the landowners.

A peasant leader's testimony

In October 1963, one year after the first agrarian reform law was signed, Villeda Morales was deposed by a military coup and a new wave of repression began. FENACH was one of its first victims; its offices in El Progreso were destroyed and its leaders imprisoned.

Marcial Caballero, later to become leader of the National Union of

Peasants, returned home from his army service to find his father, who had worked for United Fruit for thirty years, and the Caballero family of ten children evicted from the land they were working, land abandoned by United Fruit. When complaints to the National Agrarian Institute (INA) resolved nothing, Marcial Caballero and his colleagues moved back to their land with rifles and machetes. The manager of Citrus Fruit, which claimed title, had Caballero dragged off to jail and tortured. Caballero stated later:

What they didn't understand is that their efforts only made us more determined. We took over the land again, but this time we held on to it. And I went to work for the UNC, so I could help other poor people fight for their rights.[8]

Between 1962 and 1966 the state granted land to only 453 families, and they got little more than five acres apiece.[9] It was a mild and ineffectual program, which set no limit on private property as long as the holders could claim the land was in use. Still, agrarian reform was one of the supposedly "communist" measures that led to the fall of Villeda Morales.

The INA moved ahead more quickly when the surprisingly reform-minded military president, Oswaldo López Arellano, brought in Rigoberto Sandoval, a Chilean agronomist, to head the INA, and gave the organization an adequate budget at last. Sandoval favoured co-operatives like the Guanchias, formed in 1965 by out-of-work banana workers on United Fruit land that had been turned over to the INA. Guanchias was a success with the peasants, who learned the benefits of co-operative farming. It proved an advantage, too, to the fruit companies, which could buy and market Guanchias produce at no risk or expense.

But renewed activism in the INA could not give the peasants security. Landowners continued to evict tenant farmers and to respond to invasions of their "property" with force rather than wait for the INA to settle disputes. Their opposition led to formation of the National Federation of Honduran Cattlemen and Farmers (FENAGH) in 1966. FENAGH would be one of the instigating forces of the 1969 war with El Salvador.

A war over land

The war with El Salvador was triggered by violence at the World Cup soccer games, but one of its basic causes was demand for land. Another cause was the inequities of the Central American Common Market. The ecological origins have been explored by historian William H. Durham in his analysis of land-ownership in El Salvador and Honduras at the time. Almost half of El Salvador's peasantry was landless or land-poor because of rapid expansion in the export crop economy. Many drifted into Honduras until, by 1969, Salvadorans made up nearly 20 per cent of Honduras's peasant population.[10] At the same time, the Honduran population had grown precipitously, quadrupling between 1887 and 1950 and doubling between 1950 and 1974.[11] Agrarian reform was too slow to answer the demand for land. The INA found it easier to evict Salvadorans than seize fallow land from the Honduran landowners, and FENAGH also deflected pressure by blaming the Salvadorans. FENAGH insisted, "It is the foreigners who are usurping rural properties."[12]

In April 1969, Honduran authorities gave the Salvadoran settlers thirty days to get off the land, and eleven thousand Salvadorans crossed back over the border, urged along by the National Party's vigilante squad, the Mancha Brava. War broke out, lasting little more than a month before the Organization of American States imposed a ceasefire. The Honduran peasants suffered most: two thousand of them were killed and another hundred thousand were displaced as the Salvadoran army advanced deep into Honduran territory, in the middle of the growing season.

Honduras got the worst of the warfare, and one effect of its subsequent defeat was a general pressure for change, for modernization and recuperation of the nation's honour. But, when the National Party returned to power in 1971, the INA reforms ground to a halt. The peasants had become remarkably disciplined in their invasions, checking out the legal status and advising the INA before they moved onto a piece of land.[13] The landowners were not so patient. In one of FENAGH's most violent attacks, in 1975, five peasant demonstrators were killed at a UNC training centre. The bodies of nine others were discovered, burned to death in bread ovens, at the Los Horcones ranch in Olancho.[14] Thousands marched to Tegucigalpa to protest, and to demand genuine agrarian reform.

When UNC, ANACH, and a new association of co-operatives (FECORAH) united to form the Front of Campesino Unity (FUNC) that same year, the government was forced to call back Rigoberto Sandoval to lead the INA. Sandoval immediately announced the expropriation of fifty-eight thousand acres from private hands, and twenty-eight thousand from United Brands. The owners protested, Sandoval resigned, and agrarian reform returned to its snail's pace. INA staff members calculated that at the existing pace of agrarian reform it would take another 103 years to reach the goals set for agrarian reform by 1979.[15]

The trouble was not just the slowness of land redistribution; it was the lack of technical support, credit, or market access for the newly entitled peasants. Those who could not subsist on the land they acquired had to sell off their land cheap, so that the banks became the chief beneficiaries of reform.

Military assistance

In the 1970s the Honduran military played an increasing part in repression of the peasant movement. In 1977, for example, Standard Fruit called in the Fourth Infantry Battalion in La Ceiba to invade the offices of the Isletas co-operative, which had been set up with nine hundred associates on land expropriated from Standard Fruit. Supported by the INA and later by the Honduran Banana Corporation (COHBANA), Isletas was doing so well that its sales had grown to over four million boxes in 1977.

The crisis came when Isletas considered selling its bananas through the Union of Banana Exporting Countries (UPEB) instead of through Standard Fruit. Standard's response was to arrange a special assembly to elect a new Isletas leadership and to call in Lt. Col. Gustavo Alvarez Martínez, then on the company's payroll. Alvarez received $2,850 from the company just prior to raiding Isletas and arresting the board members of the co-operative, who were imprisoned for two years.[16] A new board was appointed and given military protection, while the military hunted down, tortured, and jailed nearly two hundred other co-operative members. The new management milked the Isletas capital, paid COHBANA $1 million a year for "technical assistance" and signed a long-term contract with Standard that gave them little more than half the price they had been offered by UPEB for bananas. By 1981, the INA had taken over Isletas and it ceased to function as a co-operative.

Reform – for whose benefit?

While the number of people who have benefitted from agrarian reform in Honduras (12 per cent of rural families) has been much larger than in any other Central American country, landlessness has actually increased because of the natural increase in population and the slowness of reform. In its first year of office, in 1982, the government of Roberto Suazo Córdova distributed only 40,334 acres of land, compared to almost 289,000 acres distributed at the height of land reform in 1975.[17]

Although ANACH, UNC, and FECORAH joined in a National Unity Front of Honduran Peasants (FUNACAMH) in 1979, unity fell apart in late 1984, due to corruption and dissension. Peasant mobilization became more hazardous with national security measures introduced by Col. Alvarez Martínez, who became the armed forces' chief in 1982. Decree No. 33 set five to twenty-year sentences for crimes "against rural properties", thereby legalizing renewed repression of the peasant organizations. The UNC saw 334 of its members jailed at one time or another in the following two years.[18] A related measure, passed in 1983, called all land invasions a crime, although they had been standard practice for years as the only way to get the INA to legitimize a claim.

The INA changed emphasis in 1983 from land distribution to land titling, on a model promoted by the University of Wisconsin. As marketing professor Philip Shepherd points out:

Land titling also tends strongly to individualize and divide peasants. Land titling, because of its emphasis on individual plots and property rights, encourages small farmers and peasants to eschew collective action for legal rights in favour of "possessive individualism". It has the consequence of depoliticizing the peasantry, making it easier to control and dominate.[19]

Alvarez Martínez, also president of the right-wing business group, the Association for Honduran Progress (APROH), suggested an even more reactionary plan: "social forestry co-operatives" under the jurisdiction of the Honduran military. These would in effect turn rural Honduras into an armed camp and funnel U.S. economic aid to the 4,400 large landowners as much as to the poor peasants.[20]

Neither plan provided help where it was most needed. According to Rudolfo Cortés, director of the Catholic Training Centre Las Milpas in Pinalejo, in the Department of Yoro, the peasant who does get land still starves:

The peasant who gets a little land cannot afford seeds or tools. He cannot sell at a reasonable price because he has no money to bribe the middle man so he is always in debt. Nine of the peasants here were jailed for thirteen days when they complained about waiting two years in line for land. When they eventually got the land, it was so rocky they couldn't drive a stick into it.

This country has to recognize that its peasants are not dirt; they are the nation's strength, just as land is our nation's wealth.[21]

Pressure for land reform increased with the formation in 1985 of a new, independent peasant organization, the National Congress of Rural Workers (CNTC). By 1987 the CNTC claimed twenty-four thousand members and was spearheading the land invasions.

The issue of land remains at the heart of the Honduran economic and social system, just as the Honduran peasant movement is still the most highly motivated and organized force in the nation. That truth hit home in 1987, when the plight of sixteen thousand Honduran peasants dispossessed by the Nicaraguan contra forces reached the U.S. Congress in Washington. The displaced peasants, not coincidentally, grew the bulk of the export coffee crop. The contra forces who took over their land therefore not only injured the peasants but also hurt Honduran exports. Seven thousand members of the Honduran Association of Coffee Producers (APROCAFE), demanded $13.5 million compensation and their leaders went to the U.S. Congress to back up their demands, much to the embarrassment of President José Simon Azcona Hoyo.[22] Hunger marches by displaced peasants had made no stir but, after all, in Honduras it is peasants who nurture and harvest most of the coffee – unlike El Salvador or Guatemala, where the crop is controlled by the coffee barons. In Honduras, the peasant movement could no longer be ignored.

The Catholic church and state repression

New institutions were clearly needed to represent the interests of the Honduran people. At first it appeared that the church would fulfil this role, as the Catholic church in El Salvador did through Archbishop Oscar Romero. But the church in Honduras had always been weak. It had few sanctuaries, few priests, and little wealth. By the late 1970s there were still only 232 priests, barely one for every 9,950 Catholics.[23] And only 55 of these were Honduran-born.

With priests lacking, the Catholic church passed authority over to the laity. The Delegates of the Word movement began in Honduras in 1966, and later spread to the rest of Central America. By the 1980s there were ten thousand local delegates in Honduras. At first, according to Bishop Bernardino Mazzarelli, the delegates were not warmly received: "Some people looked on them as Protestants, until finally the bishop came in person to introduce them."[24] Delegates of the Word understood local conditions and were able to work successfully at a grass-roots level. Just as importantly to an impoverished church, they received no salary.

The Catholic church complemented its lay movement with rural education through co-operatives and a chain of one hundred radio schools that reached fifteen thousand students by 1972. Out of these courses came the Social-Christian Peasant Association (ACASCH), which would later become the UNC. But it became dangerous for the clergy to involve themselves, even as mere witnesses, in the land invasions organized through ACASCH. Father Luis Henas witnessed the murder of eight peasants by the military on January 18, 1972 at Talanquera: "I began to tremble all over, seeing the massacred bodies ... and I thought of Tobias in the Old Testament who was condemned because he went at night to bury the bodies of his slaughtered fellow patriots."[25]

As violent repression against peasants increased, the Catholic church began to draw back from direct involvement with social reform. Instead, a Co-ordinating Council for Development (CONCORDE) took over its co-operatives, radio schools, and training centres, and Catholic political activists formed a forerunner of the present Christian Democrat Party. The murder of two priests at Olancho in 1975 would confirm the church's fears of confrontation with the ruling class.

Local landowners had set a price of $10,000 on the head of the local bishop and paid another $2,500 to the Olancho military commander to get rid of the local priest, Father Iván Betancur. On June 25, 1975, the military broke up a peaceful occupation of the Catholic training centre in Juticalpa and seized Father Jerome Cypher, a visiting priest from Wisconsin, driving him and five peasants to the ranch of one of the landowners, José Manuel Zelaya.

They also picked up Father Iván Betancur and two young women driving with him back from Tegucigalpa. Both priests were stripped and beaten. Cypher was castrated and shot. Betancur had his eyes gouged out, his fingernails, tongue, and teeth pulled out, his hands, feet, and testicles slashed off. The bodies of the two men were thrown down a well with those of the five peasants, and the two women were thrown in alive. The soldiers sealed the well off with a blast of dynamite. The landowners and military went on to pillage every church, convent, and parish house in the Department of Olancho, arresting or expelling thirty-two priests and nuns.

Investigation later proved that the National Federation of Cattlemen and Farmers (FENAGH) had planned the attacks with the knowledge of the Honduran government. The army officers involved got ten years in jail, but the owner of the ranch, whose son was married to President Juan Alberto Melgar's daughter, was exonerated and released.[26]

The Olancho massacre scared off the church hierarchy. Bishop D'Antonio of Olancho was relieved of his post, although he wrote to President Melgar, insisting: "What happened in Olancho is only another inducement to continue our Christian work. If the authors of the massacre were trying to intimidate the Church in its evangelical mission, they have not succeeded."[27]

Although the church hierarchy drew back, its priests, especially the Jesuit priests, continued to protest abuses of military authority. Father James Guadalupe Carney worked among the Honduran peasants from 1961 until 1978, promoting peasant organizations, until the Paz García regime expelled him and revoked his Honduran citizenship. Although Carney received no sympathy from the church hierarchy, even the conservative Honduran Bishops' Conference began to protest the repressive regime of General Gustavo Alvarez Martínez, who had suspected even the bishops of communism.[28]

Carney went to Nicaragua, but decided to return to Honduras as chaplain to a guerrilla band of the Revolutionary Party of Central American Workers (PRTC-H). The forty men crossed into Honduras in July 1983. Two months later, the Honduran military announced all of them had been killed or captured. Father Carney was said to have died of exhaustion and starvation, although his body was never produced. An investigation by journalists and by

Carney's family led to elaborate cover-ups and the mysterious deaths of witnesses who insisted Carney had been captured and later interrogated by U.S. advisers. General Alvarez himself had been seen in Olancho when the prisoners were brought to the El Aguacate air base.[29] Florencio Caballero, a former interrogator for Battalion 3-16 of the Public Security Force (FUSEP), later fled to Canada and revealed how his brigade had kidnapped, tortured, and assassinated Father Carney and many others considered to be subversives.[30]

The repression continued. In August 1985, Father Juan Donald, a Jesuit, was arrested, driven in a U.S. Army jeep to a U.S. base, then flown to San Pedro Sula and finally to Tegucigalpa, where he was interrogated by the National Department of Investigations (DNI). Two days later the U.S. consul arrived, arranged his release, and told him it was all a mistake.

In March 1986, a Canadian priest, Father William Arsenault, was murdered at Zamoranito, twenty miles east of Tegucigalpa, where he had worked for two decades for the Catholic charity, Caritas. The police immediately blamed his murder on left-wing guerrillas; later they found out the murderers were former Nicaraguans who had tried to rob him.

Although the contra war had brought a wave of violence, the Honduran bishops were reluctant to blame the United States. The Episcopal Conference refused to welcome two hundred religious women from the United States and Canada who were prevented from landing at Tegucigalpa to pray for peace in November 1983. It supported the Nicaraguan church hierarchy in its fight with the Nicaraguan government. Monsignor Muldoon, the Bishop of Olancho, the only civilian invited to the closing ceremonies of joint U.S.-Honduran military manoeuvres in 1986, declared that the exercises posed no contradiction to Christian faith. To make things quite clear, the Archbishop's office in Tegucigalpa announced, "We must all approve the presence of the marines in Honduras.... The presence of U.S. troops has, in a great part, prevented Nicaragua from invading us."[31]

Anti-Sandinista attacks by the Honduran church continued. Even when the church protested the effects of U.S. militarization (such as sexual abuse of children by U.S. troops at Palmerola), it refrained from protesting the military occupation itself.

The church did protest repression against its workers, such as the expulsion of Sister Marina from Tocoa in 1985, or the torture of Father Eduardo Méndez at Taulabe in 1986. But its chief complaint was that military persecution of the "popular church" reflected an attempt to divide the church.[32] Church unity was apparently more important than protecting church members from abuse.

Protestant complicity

The Protestant church has been even more reticent, advocating spiritual and individual solutions to the common misery and, in some cases, denouncing the efforts of Catholic workers to encourage popular organization.

Protestant sects are fairly new to Honduras. In the 1960s there were barely a dozen different denominations in Honduras, most of them in the city slums or along the Caribbean coast. By the 1980s there were more than fifty, many of them Pentecostal groups following u.s. teachings and equating both Catholicism and communism with a coming apocalypse. According to the Honduran Centre for Documentation (CEDOH), their encouragement of individual enterprise also attacks co-operative or communal organization, and they equate Delegates of the Word with "subversives".[33]

One Protestant group had greater pretensions: the Unification Church, known as the "Moonies" after its leader, the Rev. Sun Myung Moon. In 1982 the Unification Church began a massive recruitment drive. Its representative in Honduras, Col. Bo Hi Pak, became a frequent guest of President Roberto Suazo Córdova and of General Alvarez Martínez.[34] When its front organization, the Confederation of Associations for the Unity of American Societies (CAUSA), contributed $50,000 to APROH, the anti-communist business lobby presided over by Alvarez, the Catholic Episcopal Conference reacted by denouncing the "religious and moral dangers" posed by the Unification Church, and forbidding all Catholics from participating in CAUSA activities.[35] The disgrace and imprisonment of the Rev. Moon for tax evasion in the United States, and the ousting of Alvarez in 1984 ended the Unification church's campaign in Honduras.

Although at least one Protestant group, the Evangelical Mennonites, spoke up against contra abuses in 1986,[36] the newer sects, with their message of individualism and obedience, continued to ignore or actively oppose any protests against militarization or repression, rather than speak up for the victims.

10

The People Speak

"They are just a measly minority."

PRESIDENT JOSE AZCONA HOYO,
speaking of peace demonstrators, February 1987

By 1980 it was apparent that the traditional representatives of the people would not be sufficient to combat government inertia, repression, and manipulation. There would have to be popular organizations, and they would have to have practical goals and dynamic structures if they were to appeal to the essentially practical people of Honduras.

The popular organizations would develop out of failures as well as successes. Perhaps the most surprising failure was that of the student movement.

The student lesson

As early as 1910, university students had formed an organization called "Regeneration of Honduras". Successive generations of university students fought not only for university autonomy, but for the working class. For example, in 1956 students took over the San Francisco barracks in Tegucigalpa in support of demands by the unemployed.[1] Although the National Autonomous University of Honduras (UNAH) was small (only 2,600 students in 1965), its Reformist University Front led protests throughout the 1960s and 1970s, only to collapse through division. Students split between the pro-Moscow line (*los gordos*, the fat ones) and the Maoists (*los flacos*, the skinnies).

This allowed the right-wing United University Democratic Front (FUUD) to take control not only of student activities but also of the university council.

By the time the left had rejoined in 1984, the UNAH had become an elite campus, catering to the cautious middle class, and controlled by a rector, Osvaldo Ramos Soto, who was secretary of the APROH businessmen's group and a close friend of General Alvarez. Goon squads kept the lid on student activities and controlled elections. Professors were screened for leftist tendencies and books censored. Any revival in opposition to government policy would have to wait until 1987 and the revival of the university staff union, SITRAUNA. Some of the more active disillusioned students joined the armed resistance in the 1970s.

Joining the guerrillas

Guerrilla forces have been relatively small in Honduras. *The New York Times* estimated in 1987 that the guerrillas amounted to 600 members, an estimate generally considered high.[2] The five groups are:

1. The Popular Liberation Movement *"Cinchoneros"* (MPL), associated with the Communist Party and named after a peasant leader of the 1860s. The *Cinchoneros* successfully hijacked an airliner in 1982 to free political prisoners, and held eighty-three members of the San Pedro Sula Chamber of Commerce hostage the same year.

2. The Morazanist Liberation Front (FMLNH), the armed wing of the Maoist Party (PCH-ML).

3. The Popular Revolutionary Forces "Lorenzo Zelaya" (FPR), named after another peasant leader and formed by members of FENACH. It was responsible for numerous bombings in the early 1980s, and its Froylán Turcios Front claimed responsibility for two bombings in February 1987. One of these attacks was directed at the home of contra leaders. Two weeks later Honduran security forces executed a couple who they claimed were Lorenzo Zelaya leaders.[3]

4. The Revolutionary Party of Central American Workers (PRTC-H). A band of PRTC-H guerrillas, led by José María Reyes Matta, and with Father Guadalupe Carney as chaplain, entered Honduras from Nicaragua in 1983 and were almost wiped out by the military.

5. The Revolutionary Unity of the People (URP), formed in 1979. Its two leaders were murdered in June 1981, and little has been heard of the group since then.

The five guerrilla groups formed an alliance, the National Unitary Direction (DNU) in June 1983, but armed resistance gained little popular support in the following years. One Honduran social scientist explains this as a matter of timing:

Compared to the advanced state of the movement in neighboring countries, the Honduran revolutionary forces were in a formative state when the U.S. implemented its regional strategy in the early 1980s. Added to this was the wave of repression unleashed by Alvarez, which, at least temporarily, was capable of eliminating leaders and disbanding the movement.[4]

There is also criticism that the Honduran left concentrates too much on regional issues, such as the U.S. war against Nicaragua, and too little on national problems of poverty, unemployment, and hunger. Also, peasants ready to take up machetes to defend their land are by no means ready to take up arms against their government.

Where peasants and political activists do meet is on the subject of sovereignty. The U.S. war brought the contras who robbed, murdered, and displaced Honduran peasants. It was not just a resurgence of national pride that fired a mass protest; it was healthy self-interest. The issue of sovereignty united opposition forces, first through the Committee for the Defence of National Peace and Sovereignty, and then the wider Co-ordinating Committee of Popular Organizations (CCOP) that included labour and peasant groups. A leading force in CCOP has been the Committee for the Defence of Human Rights (CODEH), which has resolutely maintained that human rights go beyond the right to life and embrace the right to a decent life.

Human rights

From its start in 1981 in the modest offices of its president, Dr. Ramón Custodio, CODEH has gained international prestige and awards. It now has a large network throughout the country, and an impressive publications office. Vicious attacks from its opposition are a tribute to its effectiveness.

CODEH and Dr. Custodio, who was once imprisoned by General Alvarez for returning home with a Salvadoran "FMLN Venceremos" calendar in his possession, also came under attack from the U.S. State Department. A 1986 State Department report called CODEH "an anti-democratic leftist organization". The report cited "partisan political attacks" and "wilful exaggeration" – referring to CODEH protests against death-squad activities and a death list identifying seventeen prominent Hondurans, Custodio among them.[5] The only common denominator in the names listed was opposition to U.S. militarization and the presence of contra forces. CODEH replied indignantly that it was "putting in practice the defence and promotion of the human rights of the next generation" and was "satisfied with having political common ground with those organizations and with two-thirds of the U.S. people who are opposed to the Reagan administration's policy in Central America".[6]

Further attacks came: defamatory posters, death threats, Molotov cocktails, and finally a smoking bomb left on Custodio's desk. He ripped up some wires to neutralize it and presented the bomb to the criminal court judge.[7] In December 1987, Custodio denounced another plot against his life, planned specifically by Battalion 3-16.

On Jan. 14, 1988, Dr. Miguel Angel Pavón, northern regional director of CODEH, was murdered by armed civilians in San Pedro Sula. He was about to testify before the Inter-American Court of Human Rights, meeting in Costa Rica to consider the cases of two Hondurans and two Costa Ricans who had disappeared in Honduras in 1982. This would be the first such case against a Central American government. Two other important witnesses, police defector José Isaías Vilorio and José Lito Aguilera Córdova from the military, were murdered in the first week of January 1988, before they could testify.[8]

The CODEH case was presented jointly with the Committee of the Families of the Detained and Disappeared (COFADEH). COFADEH was begun in 1981 by Zenaida Velásquez, when her brother Manfredo, a labour activist, disappeared. She was promptly fired from her government job as a social worker and was continually harassed after that. For example, she was arrested by security forces on January 31, 1984, while waiting to meet Adolfo Pérez Esquivel, winner of the Nobel Peace Prize, at his Tegucigalpa Hotel. A wave of international protest secured her release.

COFADEH members held regular vigils close to the presidential palace throughout the 1980s, but their struggle to gain public awareness was difficult. Most Hondurans were still unwilling to believe human rights violations happened in what President Azcona called, in 1986, "an oasis of peace, where there is less violence than in any country in the world, with the possible exception of Switzerland and Costa Rica".[9]

All along the Honduran government refused to recognize any problem with human rights. A 1985 military investigation was such a whitewash that in 1987 the Inter-American Human Rights Court demanded a new investigation into 150 disappearances. But, again, the new commission set out to consult only government and military records. The reluctance to go further was based on more than fear of Honduran military wrath. To investigate military responsibility in deaths and disappearances carried the extra danger of revealing the role of the U.S. military in Honduras.

International concern, however, made it harder for Honduran authorities to discount groups like CODEH and COFADEH. Therefore, the part played by the Centre for Documentation was vital in spreading information and analysis world wide. The international prestige of its founder, Dr. Victor Meza, allowed him a certain freedom of action, and weight of authority, although he has, nevertheless, been repeatedly arrested. His name figured on the 1986 Honduran "hit list" as a "subversive".[10]

Another group adding authority to human rights concerns was the Bar Association's human rights committee, headed by former finance minister Manuel Acosta Bonilla. Its main concern was to challenge the legality of detentions, particularly on the north coast, where the scare of guerrilla activity led to a wave of repression in 1986.[11] But the committee also started to investigate prison conditions, reporting to Americas Watch in 1986 that 94 per cent of the prison population had not yet been brought to trial. One man, Guillermo Mejía Vides, died in jail; he had spent four years waiting for an appeal that proved successful, but came too late.[12]

Other respected figures joined the protest movement more actively. One was Dr. Juan Almendares, former rector to the university, who became head of the Peace Action Committee within the CCOP and a strong voice of protest against the effect of U.S. militarization on the nation's health. But in the end the numbers necessary to provide strength to the movement would come from the *patronatos*, neighbourhood organizations in the poorest parts of the cities, and from a surprisingly active force, given the nature of sexual inequality and *machismo* in Honduras: the women's organizations.

Women speak out

Although Honduran women were the very last in Latin America to get the vote (in 1954), they were active long before that in community organizing. Visitación Padilla, a teacher, co-founded the Boletín de Defensa Nacional which led the Honduran protest against invasion by U.S. Marines in 1924. She was also president of the Women's Culture Society, an organization much more political than its title suggests. Graciela García, who followed her as president, wrote the first history of the Honduran labour movement and was a labour leader for twenty years before being expelled from Honduras in 1944. She and María Luisa Medina were on the executive of the first Honduran Union Federation in 1929, and helped to draft its first demands, which included equal pay for equal work.[13]

Women organized strike support committees during the 1954 banana strike, and women textile workers went on strike in solidarity, but the country's lack of industrial development kept most Honduran women out of organized labour, condemning them to piece-work in non-unionized assembly plants, to market selling, or to domestic service.

Women in the factories were often exploited, even by the unions. So, when

289 women workers of the Hondbra Crescent Corset factory were shut out by the plant's closure in May 1983, the women who took the factory over and kept it running found themselves frozen out of the co-operative management board by the union they had appealed to for help – the ORIT-oriented FESITRANH.[14]

Honduran women have had to endure a tradition of male *machismo* that disparages their value inside and outside the home. The most crass example was the comment made by Plutarco Muñoz, president of the National Congress, when troops fired point blank at a peaceful demonstration in San Pedro Sula in 1944, leaving more than one hundred dead or dying. Muñoz denied there had been a single casualty, explaining that the blood on the sidewalks was there "because the women demonstrators must have been menstruating."[15]

Discrimination against women has both social and economic roots. Almost half of Honduran children are born out of wedlock, so many women are sole providers for families that average 8.6 children.[16] Approximately 40 per cent of the female population have no education at all. Women make up less than 25 per cent of students graduating from high school, and less than 17 per cent of the nation's lawyers and doctors.[17]

Machismo is harder to fight. Doris Mejía de Garay, elected president of her local of the electrical workers' union (STENEE) in 1973, admits:

My husband does not understand my struggle.... He understands that the struggle is important, but doesn't agree that I should be part of it. This is the tremendous barrier that prevents so many women from getting involved in struggles like the labour movement.[18]

Three women's organizations arose to combat discrimination against women. The Federation of Honduran Women's Associations, founded in 1950 to fight for women's suffrage, has since worked on other legal issues, including the Family Code. The Honduran Federation of Peasant Women (FEHMUC) was founded in 1977 with help from the Christian Democrat Party and the Social Christian movement, which had begun women's education within its peasant training courses. Now it has more than five thousand members, organized through local groups that emphasize health and education and also train women to set up their own farming or food co-operatives. It gives low-interest loans and provides assistance in accounting and co-op management.[19]

"We are not feminist in the North American sense," said FEHMUC representative Julia Saldania. "We are a critical organization, critical of how this country is run. We want to motivate and educate ourselves so that women can play a larger part in society, but first we have to tackle the very real problems that Honduran women face – malnutrition, parasites, unemployment, lack of proper shelter, schools, health clinics, electricity, roads. Many women don't even have a space to dig a toilet."[20]

Another women's group is the Visitación Padilla Committee, which takes the name of the first leader of the Women's Cultural Society. Like their namesake, committee members are in the forefront of the protest against the militarization of Honduras at the expense of much-needed health, nutrition, housing, and educational reform. They publish a monthly bulletin, named after Visitación's original publication, which protested U.S. intervention sixty years earlier, and they organize seminars, marches, and cultural events. One member, Ana Murillo, visited the U.S. early in 1987 to talk about the committee's progress and concepts:

When we had our first march in 1984 to commemorate International Nutrition Day, 50 "crazy women" came out. In 1987, to celebrate International Women's Day, 4,000 women came out.... On March 5, the peace movement organized the March for National Dignity and 10,000 people responded ...

At the beginning, 10 or 15 women would come to our seminars; now 180 to 200 attend.... We understand that not everybody reads, so we are creating radio shows with the help of student groups ...

We are creating and writing history. Historically, women have moved from a limiting environment like their parents' home to marriage, a more repressive environment where they are not allowed the right to think, to study, to work on things of their own interest. The result is that whenever they question these situations, women are seen as, and therefore sometimes feel that they are, socially maladjusted.

We are creating an environment which allows women to stop being solely machines to wash clothes and make tortillas.[21]

Ana Murillo sees the committee's success as a proof not only of women's advance, but also of the emergence of an organized movement for peace, which in turn clearly indicates to her the degree of the Honduran crisis: "It's the response of the people to the conversion of our country into a garbage dump. It is the consequence of the growing number of unemployed people and the understanding that a political line or speech is irrelevant during war time because peace is for everybody and at the time of the shooting we all die."[22]

Honduran women have acquired a reputation for speaking out, in unions, peasant organizations, and in the local *patronato*, or neighbourhood association. Their spirit has sometimes shamed male colleagues into action and sometimes disconcerted male authorities. One military officer, faced by women who had taken down a fence in order to erect a health centre, complained, "What can you do with these women who talk like battleships?"[23]

Similarly, Elvia Alvarado expressed both the combativity and patience that women bring to the opposition movement:

We campesinos are used to planting seeds and waiting to see if the seeds bear fruit. We're used to working on harsh soil. And when our crops don't grow, we're used to planting again and again until they take hold.... But it is hard to think of change taking place in Central America without there first being changes in the United States. As we say in Honduras, "*Sin el perro, no hay rabia*" – without the dog, there wouldn't be rabies.[24]

The "dog" that brought the "rabies" into Honduras did not have to scramble over the fence; the Honduran military had left the gate wide open.

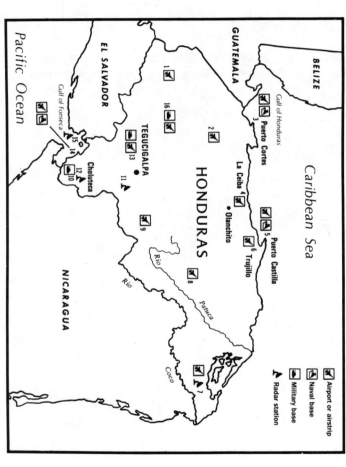

11

The Military Connection

"In effect, the Honduran armed forces are another political party and undoubtedly the strongest."

PHILIP SHEPHERD, *Honduras Confronts Its Future*

Without ever winning a war, the Honduran military managed to acquire
remarkable power. Its power came not through prestige or superior organization but through the failure of the political parties to govern effectively. This
failure allowed the military to move in and out of government, and to maintain
a crucial influence when sidelined. At the same time the armed forces attained
virtual autonomy from civil control. Finally, the U.S. militarization of Honduras gave the military precedence, even over the government or the congress.

The development of military authority came late, but so too did the development of most Honduran institutions, compared to neighbouring nations.
The military was simply "the first sector or interest group of the society to be
institutionalized".[1] The army did not in fact acquire any sense of professional-
ism until 1950, and then it was the United States that provided it. The Honduran military learned quickly and was soon able to parlay its new sense of
authority and discipline into political control. From 1954 until 1981, no chief
of the Honduran armed forces retired without having first served as president
of Honduras.

Military rule was, of course, the Central American tradition from colonial
times. Throughout the chaotic nineteenth century, a Honduran leader
needed to be as much a military man as a politician. This was as true for a
reformer like Morazán as for all other leaders. Even when there was a semblance of election rather than a coup, local militias – formed by males from age
twenty-one to thirty – ensured that the voting was conducted according to the
wishes of the local candidate for office. These local militias had no regular

training or any national allegiance. There was no concept yet of a professional army.

A new president would try to protect himself by relying on a corps of cadets. But even this corps was so undisciplined that, between 1907 and 1911, out of a total force of 279, 100 cadets deserted and 100 were released for bad conduct.[2] In the militia, things were worse. The Secretary of State complained in 1914: "Discipline ... does not exist, and for this reason, it is impossible to organize a national army."[3]

Tiburcio Carías, the dictator who started out as an army cook, began the task of creating a military apparatus, and experimented with air attacks during an unsuccessful coup in 1924. Of Carías's later aerial endeavours, journalist William Krehm commented, "In thirteen years, the only casualties from air bombardment on record were one mule and one general."[4] More important was Carías's strengthening of ties between his National Party and the military, by making his friends "Commanders at Arms" with complete regional authority and access to military support. He then called on U.S. aid to help create an army that would defend not only the country but also the presidency, should any opponent take up arms against him.

U.S. military training

The most important military training school for Central American military officers was the School of the Americas in the Panama Canal Zone. The School trained almost three thousand Honduran officers from 1946 until it closed down in 1986.[5] But the Honduran military wanted its own school, and a U.S. military mission set it up in 1947: the Francisco Morazán Military School, intended to provide a modern system of command as well as regular training. Five operative field battalions were also created, to take over from the widely dispersed, unenthusiastic, and ineffective rural militia. The United States also provided arms.

Some sort of regional defence was on the U.S. agenda and was, indeed, first proposed in 1955. Later, not surprisingly, the 1959 Cuban Revolution led to the establishment, in 1964, of the Central American Defence Council (CONDECA), designed to stop the spread of communism to the U.S. "backyard".

Earlier, the Honduran army had shown its usefulness to the United States and "regional defence" in the campaign to oust the Arbenz government in Guatemala in 1954. The round-about way in which the Hondurans were used would find a later echo in the U.S. contra war. U.S. authorities created a "ghost" army of Guatemalan rebels, trained them illegally on Honduran soil, and armed them by trumping up a threat to Honduras: a supposed shipment of

Soviet arms to Arbenz, which would have to be countered by cargos of weaponry from the United States. The U.S. Air Force shipped in the guns, ostensibly for the Honduran army to defend itself, but the arms were diverted instead to the Guatemalan "rebels". More important to U.S. efforts than local military support was the expertise of ORIT labour advisers who had been brought to Honduras after the 1954 banana strike. They were "lent" to Guatemala to purge their unions of leftist leanings – a purge so successful that union membership in Guatemala dropped from 100,000 to 27,000 in one year.[6]

The army and government

In 1957 the Honduran army emerged as a political force in its own right, as a result of the fraudulent election of Julio Lozano. Two weeks after the elections, General Roque J. Rodríguez, head of the military school, declared: "The Armed Forces of Honduras could not remain indifferent to the aspirations of the Honduran people who wished to return to a regime of order, of tranquillity and of law."[7]

Steve C. Ropp, a specialist in the study of Latin American military elites, has argued that this military takeover was a major watershed in Honduran political history, since it revealed that the military now had enough organization, cohesion, and strength to act autonomously to restore stability at a time when the two traditional parties were in chaos.[8]

The military handed back power to civilians after nineteen months, in return for a new constitution engineered by the defence minister, Lt. Col. Oscar López Arellano. The constitution gave the military virtual autonomy. The chief of the armed forces, nominated by the high command, could disobey any presidential orders that he considered unconstitutional. Military autonomy, although designed to protect the country from political irresponsibility, opened the way to increasing military involvement in government.

There were also reports of a secret meeting at the United Fruit Company's Blue Waters resort, attended by the new president Villeda Morales (1957-63), top-ranking Honduran military officers, United Fruit officials, and the U.S. ambassador. The meeting was supposedly designed to prevent the Liberal, reform-minded Villeda from turning Honduras into an Arbenz-style Guatemala.[9]

With the Cuban revolution of 1959, Central American armies gained new importance for the United States. In October 1959, the U.S. military's Caribbean Command recommended "maximizing the influence of the military in Latin America" because their loyalties were more easy to ensure than those of fickle politicians.[10] U.S. military strategy also shifted to counter-intelligence capabilities, which might have seemed appropriate to some given the growing unrest in Guatemala and El Salvador, but made little sense in the context of the much quieter Honduras.

Villeda allowed the United States to mount a radio station on Swan Island, off the northern Honduran coast, in order to broadcast anti-Castro propaganda to Cuba in 1960.[11] By allowing this use Villeda drew Honduras into a U.S.-Cuban fight and involved it in a propaganda war quite foreign to the country's realities. Honduras was soon drawn even more deeply into U.S. regional strategy. Joint U.S. and Honduran military exercises began even before creation of the Central American Defence Council in 1964. In 1962, "Operation Brotherhood" simulated defence of Tegucigalpa's Toncontín airport against mysterious foreigners.[12] CONDECA was intended to serve U.S. defence interests, but it also served Central American military forces by reinforcing their power and their autonomy. It created a Central American military network of fellow officers that seemed more at the service of the United States than of their respective nations.

However, Honduras remained for years merely a junior partner in U.S. anti-communist strategy, which made the Somoza dictatorship in Nicaragua its most important ally, and Guatemala the arena for trying out counter-insurgency techniques.

The increasing power of the military proved President Villeda's undoing. Those who put him in power were threatened by his reforms and by his attempts to combat their autonomy. In 1959, rebel officers seized the National Police headquarters, the telegraph office, and the military school. Loyal troops put down the rebellion, but the complicity of the National Police convinced Villeda that it was necessary to create a separate, two-thousand-man Civil Guard under the authority of the Ministry of Government and Justice. (As in most Central American nations, the National Police is part of the armed forces.) Friction with the military escalated. The Liberal candidate, Modesto Rodas, was accused of communist sympathies, and in 1963, ten days before elections, a coup broke out.

Col. López Arellano seized power, cementing his hold by winning a fraudulent election two years later as head of the National Party. His eight-year rule began bloodily. Many of the Civil Guard were massacred by troops while they slept in their barracks, and fighting broke out in the streets of Tegucigalpa with civilian bands taking over the city's highest building, the Hotel Prado. Armed bands appeared in the countryside, university students went on strike, and opposition forces took over a radio station to voice their opposition.

Villeda loyalists asked why the United States had not acted to defend the goverment against military attack, if CONDECA was supposed to provide mutual security. Robert McNamara, U.S. Secretary of Defense, remarked, "The United States cannot be everywhere simultaneously."[13]

The Army and the "Soccer War"

Neither CONDECA nor the United States government was of any help in the 1969 war with El Salvador. While the main causes of the war were ecological, introduction of the Central American Common Market (CACM) and persistent disputes over a common border had increased the friction between the two countries.

Honduras joined the CACM in 1961, at a time of industrial regional expansion, but the growth in Honduras was mostly in U.S.-owned industries, so that the Honduran nation saw little benefit while its neighbouring nations flourished. By 1967, Honduras was paying between 25 and 100 per cent more for products it imported from CACM neighbours than for those it imported from outside Central America. It was also losing $15 million a year on balance of payments.[14]

Disputes over forty-two square kilometres of land along the Río Negro between Honduras and El Salvador had been festering for 130 years. When mass expulsions of Salvadoran peasants took place at the beginning of June, El Salvador and Honduras were about to meet in soccer matches to decide which team would represent the region at the 1970 World Cup. Tempers erupted at the games, igniting a war that had much more serious causes and a serious outcome: two thousand deaths and the displacement of another hundred thousand people.

El Salvador cabled the Inter-American Commission on Human Rights to complain about "violations of human rights, with the character of genocide, such as murder, persecution, aggression, damage to property and massive expulsions.".[15] Honduras complained to the same Commission about attacks on Honduran citizens at the soccer match. Diplomatic relations were broken off, mediators from the Commission failed to get agreement, and, on July 14, El Salvador attacked six points on the Honduran frontier and bombed ten cities, including Tegucigalpa. The attacks lasted ten days and took the Salvadoran army fifteen miles inside Honduran territory.

Although the Honduran air force scored one success, destroying the Salvadoran oil refinery at Acajutla, the Honduran army was routed. The Organization of American States imposed a cease-fire and a return to previous borders.

Curiously, the Honduran military emerged from the defeat stronger than ever. The older, traditional officers were blamed for glaring inefficiencies: the antique guns, the lack of maps. But the army's inglorious role in general became mythologized as heroism and the younger officers gained power. A new spirit of nationalism arose out of defeat, but neither the National nor the Liberal party was able to take advantage of a common desire for national unity. The election of Ramón Ernesto Cruz, a Nationalist president who proved wildly unpopular, offered the military another opportunity to take power and "rescue" the nation from labour unrest. For the next nine years, Honduras was under military rule, beginning with military reform in the style of the Peruvian experiment, but moving steadily towards repression.

A Pentagon Republic

In the 1970s most U.S. attention in Central America went to Nicaragua, where Somoza was fighting to stave off revolution. But President Jimmy Carter, elected in 1976, did not neglect Honduras. From 1978 to 1980, Honduras got by far the largest share of economic and military aid in the Central American region: $127.9 million compared to $71.1 million to Nicaragua.[16] Washington leased ten Huey UH-1H helicopters valued at over $1 million each to Honduras to back up U.S.-trained border patrols intended to stop arms entering El Salvador. In March 1980, President Policarpo Paz García visited Washington, and *Washington Post* columnist Jack Anderson revealed the new role chosen for Honduras:

The President seems determined to add still another sorry chapter to the chronicle of Yankee imperialism in Central America. The administration apparently has chosen Honduras to be our new "Nicaragua" – a dependable satellite bought and paid for by American military and economic largesse.

In secret meetings with the Pentagon's emissary ... the Honduran military junta was told specifically that it is expected to assume the regional role played for years by Nicaragua's Anastasio Somoza – to become the bulwark of anticommunism against the pressure of popular revolt.[17]

The first role planned for the Honduran army was to back up the Salvadoran army's fight against the guerrillas of the Farabundo Martí Front for National Liberation (FMLN), under the pretext that supplies were reaching the FMLN from Nicaragua through Honduras. What Honduran forces did do was help in the massacre of fleeing Salvadoran peasants at the Sumpul River in 1980, and the Lempa River in 1981.[18]

General Alvarez and Ambassador Negroponte

By 1981 Honduras was preparing for presidential elections at the urging of the United States. Rather than weaken military power, a civilian government would enhance it, as both Liberal and National party candidates courted the military, and the United States relied on those it trusted to carry out the primarily military role it had picked out for Honduras. Choice of head of the armed forces would be just as important as choice of president. Although he was a mere colonel, Gustavo Alvarez Martínez was the obvious man.

Alvarez spoke fluent English. He had studied in Argentina, Panama, Peru, and Washington, and was so thoroughly imbued with the National Security Doctrine that he put Chilean dictator Augusto Pinochet's *Geopolitics* at the top of his reading list.[19] As head of the Fourth Infantry Battalion in La Ceiba in 1977, he had been on the Standard Fruit payroll and had sent in his men to invade Las Isletas co-operative. When he moved to San Pedro Sula in 1979, he ordered his police to storm the Lindo textile factory during a strike. When he became chief of the Public Security Forces (FUSEP) and the secret police (DNI) in 1980, a wave of disappearances and torture ensued.

Alvarez was convinced he was fighting a holy war. He believed, as he stated, "There are only two types of politicians – communists and others" and "Everything you do to destroy a Marxist regime is moral".[20] He saw the Sandinistas as puppets of the Soviet Union and warned: "Only when El Salvador has fallen, and Honduras and Guatemala follow, only when all of Central America is Communist, when it is already too late, will we realize the importance of this war to the death."[21]

The way had been prepared for a man like Alvarez to have a free hand. Two months before elections, the military high command met leaders of the National and Liberal parties and won the promise of no civilian interference in national security matters, and also no investigation into military corruption. Alvarez had already quarrelled with the Nationalist candidate, Ricardo Zuniga. His friendship with Liberal candidate and future president, Roberto Suazo Córdova, would benefit them both. Suazo Córdova broke army rules to promote Alvarez, a mere colonel, to lead the high command. (COSUFA), legitimizing his ascent by making him brigadier-general.

Alvarez strengthened his control by centralizing the command structure and getting for himself the titles not only of Minister of Defence but also of Commander-in-Chief, a position that had previously been the president's.[22]

Two months before Alvarez took office, the man really in charge of Honduras had arrived: John Dimitri Negroponte, the U.S. ambassador. President Suazo Córdova got a four-page letter from Negroponte handed to him at his inauguration ceremonies. The letter presented a twelve-point program of "suggestions" he should follow. For the next two years, Negroponte and Alvarez took full charge of Honduran affairs, using the president to get their policies rubber-stamped by a compliant congress. In return, Honduras

Battalion 3-16: The Death Squad

Alvarez set up an elaborate security system, including a military death-squad, Battalion 3-16. Two Honduran defectors, now living in Canada, have described how Battalion 3-16 operated. Florencio Caballero, an admitted interrogator, testified before the Inter-American Human Rights Court. José Valle López, an admitted torturer, was interviewed for a CBC television program that aired in January 1988. Both concurred on the ferocity of operations, the innocence of most victims, and the involvement of U.S. officials in planning and carrying out operations.

Valle: I was a member of Battalion 3-16 from 1981 to 1984. Once you are in, it is very difficult to get out. I worked in the kidnapping squad. We worked as a team. I would guess we were responsible for eighty or ninety deaths out of nearly two hundred, most of them innocent civilians. At first we were told to drop any kids we kidnapped in the park; later, we were told to kill them, too. And instead of shooting, we were told to use machetes or knives. For torture sessions, we used electric shocks, the hood, and the bucket, filled with stones, hung from a victim's testicles. And the bodies were buried secretly. I have told Amnesty and Americas Watch some of the cemeteries and the secret jails.

A Mr. Mike from the U.S. Embassy sat in on many torture sessions and provided written questions. We handed over all documents to three U.S. women in charge of documentation.

There were other gringos, too, with special equipment when we went on auto patrols. We even took American pseudonyms. I was Peter and my boss, Lt. Marco Tulio Regalado Hernández, was "Ronnie".

Source: interview with author, Toronto, February 1988.

became, in 1982, the second largest recipient of U.S. military aid in Latin America, receiving $31.3 million, which was slightly more than it had received for the whole period from 1946 to 1981.

Massive U.S. manoeuvres began, not merely to intimidate the Sandinistas but moreover to provide cover for the secretly-financed contra war against the Sandinista government in Nicaragua. Exercises purporting to train the Honduran army escalated out of all proportion. On November 8, 1982, *Newsweek* blew the lid off what it called "America's Secret War – Target Nicaragua".[23] Revelations of covert activities and contra atrocities began to mount, but the exercises continued and the map of Honduras changed, as U.S. National Guardsmen built roads and landing strips for U.S. benefit.

Once having rented its territory, Honduras had little control. U.S. troops could fly into the Palmerola base, not far from Comayagua, without customs or immigration procedures, so that the government had no way of knowing how many U.S. troops it was "hosting", or what happened to the enormous quantity of armaments brought in for military exercises. In 1980 there were twenty-five U.S. military personnel in Honduras. By 1984 there was a regular presence of some one thousand, and between 1983 and 1987 over seventy thousand U.S. troops arrived for special training.

In May 1983 troops disembarked at Puerto Castillo to set up the Regional Military Training Centre (CREM) for Salvadoran troops, before the Honduran Congress had even heard of the unconstitutional agreement Alvarez had signed with the United States. Even then, the deputies obligingly signed when Alvarez assured them it was legal; the Salvadoran troops were, of course, students, not soldiers.

Through the heady days of open U.S. funding for the contras, Alvarez flourished. The U.S. ambassador Negroponte was his friend – just so long as Alvarez lent his military intelligence officers as liaison with the contras and funnelled arms to the contras through Honduran military accounts. In May 1983 Alvarez was invited to Washington to receive the U.S. Legion of Merit. When the U.S. Congress began to draw back from contra funding, Alvarez put the contras in touch with his friend Ariel Sharon, Israeli defence minister, and set up channels for arms later used by the "contragate" conspirators.[24]

But Alvarez was proving too much of a wild card. In December 1983, he boasted he would be in Managua on his next birthday; several times he had to be held back from initiating direct attacks on the Nicaraguan army. His enthusiasm for the Unification Church, the Moonies, was also an embarrassment. A gift of $50,000 from the Moonies' political wing, CAUSA, went to the Association for Honduran Progress (APROH), the business group Alvarez headed. The Catholic members of APROH and the Honduran Catholic church were duly upset, especially when the Rev. Sun Myung Moon ended up in a U.S. jail for tax evasion.

The end came for Alvarez from his own officers, who were outraged by his efforts to reduce the high command (COSUFA) from forty-five to twenty-one and forestall his rivals by raising the minimum age for generals. There was also the little matter of a missing $1 million intended for arms purchases.

The first person to hear about an intended coup was Ambassador Negroponte, who made no remonstrance. On March 31, 1984, Alvarez was seized when he was about to return from San Pedro Sula, and hustled off instead, handcuffed, aboard a jet for Costa Rica. When President Suazo Córdova demurred, he was told, "The plane is still waiting. You can join him."[25]

After Alvarez

General Walter López Reyes, who succeeded Alvarez, was either unable or unwilling to stop U.S. militarization, although he did stop the training of Salvadoran troops in 1985. López represented typical, rather than rabid Honduran military attitudes. He moderated the army's stance, toned down the anti-Sandinista threats and gave some encouragement to the rising nationalism emerging from wide sectors of Honduran society. Much more of a politician than Alvarez, he pleased the army by pressing for more military aid, including a dozen U.S. jets, while trying to establish new terms for the 1954 treaty that allowed the United States a free hand in military manoeuvres. But his trip to Washington with President Suazo Córdova in 1985 to get further aid was singularly unsuccessful. Earlier agreements and a host of secret payoffs prevented any bail-out from the U.S. war against Nicaragua.

The worst excesses of the security forces abated somewhat when López took over, but it is significant that he did not dismantle the secret intelligence unit, Battalion 3-16, a fact that later came to light in testimony by a former interrogator. In fact, one of his officers, Major Ricardo Zúñiga, a liaison between the Honduran Army and the U.S. Embassy, travelled six times to Washington during López's term in office, to reveal CIA and contra links to more than two hundred Honduran murders and kidnappings. Zúñiga was promptly cashiered and arrested. His body was found in September 1985, in the Department of Olancho close to the border, the territory that contras call "new Nicaragua".[26]

López's best efforts were as a political mediator during the last shoddy days of the Suazo Córdova presidency, when he persuaded a reluctant president not to cling to power and held back the military from bringing on a coup. But he was, in turn, out-foxed. Five days after the election of President José Simon Azcona Hoyo, a particular foe of Suazo Córdova, López was out. He was pressured to resign, some say, by a vindictive former president, but was also eased out by jealous fellow officers who acted smartly on his offer of resignation, denying him any second thoughts.

Rather than stir through the murk of military rivalries between different promotion years, it is more fruitful to notice how such influential changes in command are made in Honduras without any civilian say. The military keeps its own counsel and answers to no civilian authority, because the commander-in-chief has relative autonomy. The National Congress was never consulted about either the removal of Alvarez or the resignation of López.

The new man, navy chief Humberto Regalado Hernández, was much more of a creature of the military command than an ambitious politician. He told interviewers that he endorsed U.S. manoeuvres and that military relations with the United States would become closer under his command.[27] Indeed, the war games vastly increased. The 1987 Solid Shield exercise involved fifty thousand U.S. troops, many of them members of the National Guard. Thousands of Marines "invaded" the beaches close to Puerto Castilla in imitation of the 1983 Grenada invasion. The purpose of the gigantic military exercise, according to the U.S. Embassy, was "to simulate response to a petition from a friendly nation to help it repel an attack from a neighboring country".[28]

Between October 1981 and February 1983, there were five military exercises, including the first large-scale involvement of U.S. army, navy, and air force personnel – Ahuas Taras (Big Pine) I and II. Between August 1983 and August 1987, there were fifty. Although the Honduran government was not privy to their planning, this seemed of little concern to President Suazo Córdova, who stated: "May there not only be Ahuas Taras II, but many Ahuas Taras – three, four, five and six as long as I am president – to train our armed forces, to bring the United States and Honduras closer together."[29]

Spoils and squabbles

The war games made less and less pretence of training the Honduran army. Honduran soldiers resented having to sit on one side with their rice and beans while the U.S. allies enjoyed cold beer and steak on manoeuvres. Honduran military commanders also resented the fact that U.S. troops and the contra forces came first. It also appeared to be turning into a long-term situation, as U.S. installations were entrenched. The Palmerola air command, for example, was to be redesigned to last another fifteen years.

Tired of playing second fiddle, the Honduran military took advantage of all the possibilities for gain. There will never be a thorough accounting of the arms that passed to the contras through the joint war games, or of the arms signed for by the Honduran military and then passed to the contras, although some facts surfaced during the 1987 Tower Commission hearings. Rumours led to counter-charges of corruption involving former Honduran military chiefs Alvarez and López. Alvarez had undoubtedly feathered his nest, from his APROH position as well as his military command. There was talk that he took $30 million with him when he left. He lashed out in turn at López, when U.S. Congressional reports showed over $1 million in contra aid diverted to the Honduran military during López's term of office (May 1984 to Jan. 30,

1986).[30] There was also the little matter of $30 million missing in contragate funds, which the rebels insisted they never saw, and the payoffs for the six shiploads of Israeli arms for the contras that went through Honduras between 1985 and 1986.[31] With so many sticky fingers in so many secret accounts, we will probably never know the truth.

Within Honduran circles, the squabbles descended to gangster levels. For example, an alternate congress depty, Rodolfo Zelaya, reported in August 1986 that two colonels had raided his home. He accused Lt. Col. Roberto Núñez Montes of trying to muscle in on his lucrative contra-supply operations. Col. Núñez was suspended but later reinstated by a military commission.[32]

Such criminality exemplified the way U.S. militarization encouraged the worst in Honduran military behaviour. Instead of turning the Honduran military into a force that could ensure Honduran peace and security, the U.S. connection and influence had increased the military's political power, encouraged its abuse of human rights, and catered to its veniality. The Honduran army had become on the one hand more of a threat to Honduran democracy, and on the other more of a stooge in the U.S. war.

12

Losing Out in the U.S. War Games

"We can't have development and militarization at the same time. We can either feed soldiers or feed children."

DR. JUAN ALMENDARES, *Food First Alert*

By the mid-1980s priorities imposed by U.S. foreign policy had overshadowed all national Honduran concerns. The nation had become USS Honduras. Philip L. Shepherd lists the tragic consequences:

Heightened regional instability, terrorist attacks on Honduras, pillage by the CIA-backed contras, marginalization of Honduran civilian leadership, increased internal repression and human rights abuses, severe economic deterioration and the postponement of urgently needed socioeconomic reforms.[1]

In the midst of this degradation, Honduran politicians kept up the pretence that there were no contras, that the war games were for the benefit of Honduran troops, that the United States was, after all, good old Uncle Sam, and that the problems of the nation were solvable by national effort. For example, at an international conference on Honduras, convened by Florida International University in November 1984, only two out of some twenty Honduran participants addressed the issue of U.S. militarization.[2]

Refusal to admit involvement in the U.S. war necessitated years of lies about the contra presence. Even when Honduran newspapers published photographs, in 1985, of a contra training camp five hundred yards from the Francisco Morazán Military School in Tegucigalpa, its presence was denied, in significant order: first by the U.S. ambassador, then by the Honduran armed forces chief, and finally by the Honduran president.[3] Honduras had agreed not only to host the contras but also to hide them.

For years, there were few complaints. Most Hondurans did not see the contras, hidden away in Danli, or the first G.I.s at Palmerola, and the United States had promised to pour down dollars on Honduras in return for sheltering the contras. By the time paratroopers were descending like rain, and contras were dispossessing peasants from their own homes, there was no drawing back.

But to blame Honduran subservience entirely on U.S. pressure would be to ignore Honduran responsibility. A history of compliance and corruption allowed U.S. militarization to take place. Honduran authorities made a bargain with the devil, but it was not for the first time. It is also delusive although dramatic to point, as some do, to a sudden and great shift in the Honduran situation. U.S. Senator James Sasser, for instance, reported to Congress in 1985, "Honduras, where democracy had once begun to flourish, has become an armed camp."[4] But others argue that true democracy, something more than ritual elections and two political parties, had yet to be implanted. Likewise, the theory that Honduras was "an oasis of peace" amid regional conflicts has also been disproved by history. In the end U.S. intervention merely encouraged the worst features of Honduran society and discouraged the best, building on a process of economic intervention begun one hundred years earlier.

First casualty: human rights

Although Honduras experienced its share of anti-union violence, the murder and torture of peasants, and even a few massacres, these events tended to be excesses of a particular moment, unlike the systematic policy of repression introduced by General Alvarez as part of his National Security Doctrine philosophy. But in 1981 human rights violations in Honduras increased dramatically. In 1980 there had been one political assassination; in 1981 there were forty-two. In 1980 there were two disappearances; in 1981 there were fifty-two.[5] Altogether, in the Alvarez years, there would be 214 political assassinations, 110 disappearances, and 1,947 illegal detentions.[6]

U.S. influence was obvious from the start. Many of the first victims were Salvadorans suspected of sympathy with the rebel Farabundo Martí National Liberation Front (FMLN). Later, contra Nicaraguans were among the perpetrators. Anti-communist doctrines then spread to the repression of purely local discontent.

A series of decrees institutionalized the use of force. One was the Anti-Terrorism Decree of 1982, which set down jail sentences of twenty years or more for the "subversive" act of land takeovers, which had been a traditional tactic in Honduras for years. Another Alvarez specialty, the creation of a "hot line" for spying, the Centre of Emergency Information, was more in line with counter-insurgency tactics in Argentina, where Alvarez had trained.

Once in place, repression did not cease when Alvarez left the country. In fact, the Committee for the Defence of Human Rights in Honduras (CODEH) reported an increase in the number of persons kidnapped or tortured in the following year, 1985.[7] While the Lireral government tried to deflect protests and blame it all on the General, Alvarez argued in response that everything he did had presidential approval, and indeed there is no evidence that anyone in the government opposed his measures. Alvarez's successor would leave; so would U.S. ambassador Negroponte and his successor, but human rights violations continued and became more closely aimed at those opposing the contra war.

For example, Isidro García España, a well-known Honduran actor, officiated as master of ceremonies for an anti-contra demonstration in Tegucigalpa on March 5, 1987. One hour later he was pulled out of a café by FUSEP (Public Security Force) police, dragged off, and beaten so badly that his left foot was broken and he had to be hospitalized. "That's for going on the march!" his captors told him. He was released only after pressure from the Human Rights Commission.[8]

The United States was linked directly to FUSEP interrogations and murders by the testimony of former interrogator Florencio Caballero, who defected in 1986. He told Americas Watch, an organization established in 1981 to monitor human rights in the Western Hemisphere, that the intelligence group Battalion 3-16, set up by Alvarez, had carried out more than 175 kidnappings and executions between 1980 and 1984, with advice from the CIA and assistance from a U.S. official he identified as a "Mister Mike" working out of the U.S. Embassy. Caballero said he and another twenty-four Hondurans had received six months of training in Houston, Texas, from Argentine, Chilean, and U.S. instructors. According to Caballero, although the U.S. advisers in Honduras discouraged physical torture, they knew it was going on. Caballero also gave information on the capture of fifteen Honduran guerrillas in Olancho in 1983, among them the U.S. Jesuit priest Father Guadalupe Carney. Honduran army officers had claimed that Carney was already dead from starvation and exhaustion when they found his body. According to Caballero, a very much alive Carney was taken away by air force helicopter for interrogation – and then never seen again.[9]

Caballero said that not only were there contras working within Battalion 3-16, but that they also had their own death-squads. Retired General Walter López blamed all killing on the contras, claiming that the Honduran military was helpless to stop it. He told CBS's Mike Wallace: "It was too dangerous for us to get inside the problem because if you find out who was shooting all these people you might get shot, you know."[10]

But the killings spread beyond political motivation. During the first six months of 1986, forty-five bodies were deposited in the San Pedro Sula morgue. Corpses of another fifteen "thieves" held by the National Department of Investigations (DNI) in Tegucigalpa appeared in July alone, and the Human Rights Commission reported that Battalion 3-16 was making war on anyone it considered "undesirable".[11]

Second casualty: democracy

As abuses increased, respect for civil authority disintegrated. It was part of a decline in the democratic process, which U.S. militarization was supposedly trying to protect. After all, Langhorne Motley, Assistant Secretary of State for Inter-American Affairs, had proudly announced in 1984: "In part because of U.S. support, Honduras today is clearly more progressive and more democratic than it was before the 1980s."[12] It didn't seem that way in 1987. No attempts had been made to prevent security excesses or to make fundamental changes in the political and military structures, such as creating an independent Supreme Court or separating the police force from military authority.

Hondurans looked back to the 1981 elections, when Roberto Suazo Córdova won by a hundred thousand votes and an editorial in the liberal newspaper *El Tiempo* proclaimed: "It is a vote against corruption and the presence of the military in power, a vote in favour of a change in political style and of neutrality in the regional war."[13]

Within two years, another editorial, in the liberal-centrist paper *La Tribuna,* accused the government of "spinning its wheels, inventing enemies or creating fears that have seriously divided or paralysed its executive".[14] The paper cited Suazo Córdova's personal dictatorship, government subordination to the military, the weakening of popular organizations, the collapse of legal securities, corruption, and the undermining of Liberal party democracy. It complained that the people whom the President consulted were the U.S. ambassador and General Alvarez.

Deputies in the Honduran Congress were left out of any significant role in decision-making. Efraín Díaz Arrivillaga, a Christian-Democrat deputy, reported: "The great problems that afflict Honduran society, namely problems of human rights, foreign policy and the economy are rarely debated in the Congress. The Congress legitimises all the executive wants."[15]

Congress finally revolted in 1985, when Suazo Córdova attempted to engineer another term in office and, when that failed, tried to hang on to control of the National Electoral Tribunal, which would have allowed him to pick a successor. When Congress fired the Supreme Court president for corruption and appointed a replacement, Suazo Córdova put this new judge in jail and charged more than fifty deputies with treason. It took the U.S. ambassador and General López to get him to back down. Such incidents damaged Honduras's reputation internationally, but were becoming commonplace to most Hondurans. Bishop Luis Alonso Santos of Santa Rosa de Copán commented: "Our leaders are only concerned with themselves and ignore the country's problems. Envy has produced rancor ... but the people give no importance to the bickering of those in power."[16]

Bickering continued until the November 1985 elections, as Suazo Córdova did everything he could to prevent a victory by José Azcona Hoyo, who had been his minister of communications. In this election, for the first time in Honduran history, there were a total of nine presidential candidates: four from the Liberal Party, three from the National Party, one from the Christian Democrat Party, and one from the Innovation and Unity Party. The election also included 132 members of Congress and 284 mayors. The Liberal party won, at 49 per cent of the total vote, with the National Party close behind with 43 per cent. In the curious world of Honduran politics, where the top candidate in the winning party gets the presidency, Azcona, with only 26 per cent of the vote, won out over the National Party's Rafael Leonardo Callejas, who had 41 per cent. The Liberals, without a clear majority, formed a "Unity Pact" with the Nationalists and Azcona handed them some plum cabinet jobs, including the foreign ministry.

Weaker than ever

José Azcona Hoyo had wanted to be president ever since first grade, but he had few political gifts. Unlike Suazo Córdova's folksy but foxy style, Azcona was aloof and ineffectual. With very little power in a Congress stacked with Nationalists, he was forced to make a pact with the opposition and hand them crucial offices, including that of president of the Congress. Nor could he afford to pick a fight with the army. But his Unity Pact soon broke up as every sector of Honduran society tired of his failures to achieve any new boost to the economy or to the wounded national pride. He was heavily criticized at the end of his first year in office, with the harshest criticism coming from organized labour and the peasants.[17] But his most striking failure, perhaps, was his abject compliance with the White House over the Nicaraguan "invasion that never was" in March 1986.

Third casualty: sovereignty

On the eve of a U.S. Senate vote over $100 million in contra aid, the U.S. defence department sprang news of an invasion of Honduran territory by fifteen hundred Nicaraguan troops. Both the Honduran armed forces and Azcona's office denied the report, and a *New York Times* editorial, on March 27, bore the headline, "The danger is not to Honduras". Later investigation quoted U.S. chargé d'affaires Shepard Lowman as telling Honduran officials: "We are here to help you and you are going to leave us hanging in Washington."[18]

Nevertheless, after a talk with the U.S. ambassador, Azcona phoned President Reagan to ask (as the ambassador told him to do) for urgent aid. In response Azcona got $20 million to ferry troops to what was merely a routine border-crossing by Nicaraguan military chasing the contras back to camp. But the incident was enough to provide Senate approval for Reagan's contra funds. The next day the Honduran press reproduced a *Miami Herald* editorial that called the deal "extortion" and also printed a statement by Nicaraguan President Daniel Ortega concluding that Honduras had now lost all pretence at sovereignty.[19]

A remarkably similar ploy was used almost two years later, on March 18, 1988, when the U.S. administration once again responded to a "personal phone call" from Azcona, asking for help following reported incursions by Nicaraguan troops into Honduran territory. This time, as a "friendly gesture", Reagan sent 3,200 troops into Honduran territory. Critics called the move yet another manoeuvre to win support for contra aid, an obvious attempt to disrupt Nicaraguan peace talks, and a violation of the Arias Peace Accord. The troops soon left, but questions remained about the possible "political fallout". Both Honduran and foreign diplomats maintained that the crisis was manipulated or even planned by the United States. Honduran political analyst Victor Meza commented: "The arrival of U.S. troops to the rescue like Superman could damage the respect for the Honduran military inside Honduras."[20]

Other actors in the contra farce had begun to speak out about U.S. intervention. Former ambassador John Ferch revealed that he had been removed in July 1986 because the U.S. administration "wanted somebody strong enough and pro-consul enough so that no Honduran government would object to anything".[21] Former armed forces chief Wálter López not only admitted Honduran army involvement in contra corruption, but also called the contras "mercenaries" who had no hope of victory.[22] Honduras was seen not only as being co-opted, but also – and worse – as being co-opted to a losing cause.

In Honduras protests against U.S. militarization started to come from every side, from Congress and the Liberal Party, as well as from the street. It wasn't just the contra presence being criticized; it was the U.S. presence. Traditional and religious groups became irate when reports came in of child prostitution and AIDS in Comayagua, close to the U.S. air base at Palmerola. In May 1985, there were only three AIDS cases; in 1986 there were twelve, and another seventeen in the first six months of 1987. Eight of the thirty-two cases involved female prostitutes.[23]

Honduras was rapidly becoming polarized. It did not help when armed forces chief Regalado accused all those who opposed the Reagan policy of being communists out to destroy the moral and spiritual ties of the Republic.

Critics began to question the bargain they had made with the United States, when the disadvantages showed clearly and the advantages failed to appear. Where was the promised rain of dollars? More money seemed to be going to the old enemy of Honduras, El Salvador, and to President Reagan's pets, the contras, than to compliant Honduras. Indeed, the economic situation would get worse instead of better, with increased U.S. intervention.

Fourth casualty: the economy

Honduras was in dire economic straits when Roberto Suazo Córdova took office in January 1982. State capitalization had produced horrendous debts, such as the $300 million owed by the State Investment Corporation (CONADI). The country's foreign debt represented half the Gross Domestic Product. The economy had also been hit by falling world prices for its main exports, coffee and bananas. Private investors moved their money elsewhere. Between 1979 and 1982, about $600 million left the country in private investment, most of it going to Miami, where more than five hundred Hondurans kept bank accounts.[24] Prices were rising, and so was unemployment, while production was falling. It was therefore no wonder that Gustavo Alfaro, economic minister in 1982, lamented, "Only God can save the national economy."[25]

The United States, the International Monetary Fund (IMF), and the World Bank were more readily available. Before taking office, President Suazo Córdova had sought advice from local business interests, the same men who would later form the Association for Honduran Progress (APROH) under the leadership of General Alvarez. They advised turning Honduras into another Taiwan or South Korea by creating free ports and encouraging assembly plants, offering low wages and freedom from taxes. The IMF suggested that even this change would not be enough; Honduras would have to cut back social services. The Reagan memorandum handed to President Suazo Córdova at the Honduran leader's inauguration gave the same advice.

Within two years, Honduras implemented most of the Reagan "suggestions", such as increasing investment incentives and cutting social programs. But the promised miracle failed to occur. On July 18, 1983, Suazo Córdova wrote in desperation to President Reagan:

The austerity measures are contributing toward increasing unemployment. We greatly fear that if this situation continues it will become a politically destabilizing factor and weaken our people's belief in the capacity of the democratic system to resolve the problems that we are trying to remedy through these economic policies. If we do not have the necessary outside support, these measures will have exactly the opposite political results from what we are aiming for....

Our people are beginning to ask themselves, openly and with increasing force, if our own best interests are being served by being so intimately aligned with the United States when we receive so little in return. We estimate that the requested budgetary assistance represents, in the long run, a relatively low cost when one takes into account the political and military risks that Honduras is assuming.[26]

The Honduran president asked the U.S. government for $500 million, over five years. He got $2.3 million to start, only 9.5 per cent of the total U.S. aid allotted to the region.[27] From then on Suazo Córdova ran to Washington for periodic handouts. Military aid rose much faster than economic aid, and the money spent on U.S. war games was highest of all.

It was galling for Honduran authorities to have to hand over the agreed money for gas used by U.S. troops in their war games, while getting so little reward for their "hospitality". And it was soon obvious that militarization was no gift, but an economic burden. Azcona said so himself in 1984: "We are attempting to operate a war economy when we are bankrupt."[28]

The economy continued to slide downhill. In 1986, Ortez Colindres, former president of the Central American Bank of Economic Integration, announced that "only a crazy person would dare to invest in Honduras",[29] citing the contras and U.S. military presence as factors keeping investors away. The free port facilities at Puerto Castilla stood empty. The presence of a war situation clearly made investors nervous, fearful that they could not create a Hong Kong in what seemed to be becoming another Vietnam.

In 1986, economist Antonio Murga Frassinetti calculated that the nation's total debt, repayable in foreign currency, stood at $2,502 million. If interest rates remained the same and no more money was borrowed, service charges alone to 1989 would amount to $2,579 million, almost equivalent to total revenue.[30] In January 1987, the International Development Bank showed that per capita economic growth had been negative, despite U.S. financial aid. Private investment had contracted 65 per cent in four years and the deficit in the balance of goods and services amounted to 12 per cent of the Gross Domestic Product.

The Honduran Centre for Documentation (CEDOH) analyzed the IDB reports and concluded that the $1,252 million received in U.S. aid since 1980, "instead of initiating the promised start-up to the stagnant Honduran economy, had left it in a state worse than ever".[31] It had also exacerbated poverty, unemployment, and general social disorder.

Fifth casualty: social harmony

As CEDOH pointed out, unemployment had gone up 61.2 per cent from 1980. The minimum wage was down 25 per cent in real terms for non-agricultural workers. Education and health budgets had fallen while the defence budget was up by almost 50 per cent.

Much of the economic decline was, indeed, common to the whole of Central America, as the regional conflicts skewed local economics towards defence, discouraged investment, and prevented most inter-regional trade. But the crisis hit Honduras particularly hard, because of its bare margin of economic stability. Foreign aid encouraged corruption, made the few rich even richer, and increased dependency. Austerity programs implemented to please the international banks endangered the social fabric. As former finance minister Manuel Acosta complained in 1984: "The cutbacks are bringing the population to a point of desperation. My worry is that we are, in fact, provoking a situation of violence and internal rebellion by our very neglect of these basic needs of the people."[32]

Three years later the situation was worse. There were hunger marches to the capital, and strikes for a reasonable wage. Clinics and schools closed for lack of supplies or money to pay staff. Glue-sniffing was rampant among Tegucigalpa's street kids, who could not shine shoes because that was now the job of grownups who could find no other work.

Foreign magazines carried articles about "ten lemp alley" in Comayagua, near the Palmerola base, where the going price for a prostitute was five dollars. According to Dr. Juan Almendares of the National Autonomous University, Comayagua's prostitute population numbered more than three thousand – almost 60 per cent of the total number of prostitutes in the country as a whole.[33]

To those that have not

As if its own problems were not enough, Honduras also had to shoulder the burden of 170,000 illegal immigrants, about 5 per cent of the country's total population, and all looking for work and food.[34] This was in addition to forty thousand refugees within camps run by the United Nations High Commission for Refugees. They came from El Salvador, Guatemala, and Nicaragua.

First came the Salvadorans, twenty-one thousand of them by the end of 1986, kept in barrack-like camps, denied the right to work or to move, and unable to return to their own country for fear of persecution. Their plight aroused the concern of international human rights groups and the ire of the Honduran military, who raided the camps and caused a number of deaths in their zeal to unearth FMLN guerrilla sympathisers. Another five hundred refugees came from Guatemala, but the bulk came from Nicaragua: sixteen thousand Miskitos and eight thousand ladinos, whose camps provided a home base for contra activity and endangered Honduran peasants. In spite of some repatriations, the numbers continued to rise. During June 1987, another 1,146 arrived. Most of them, according to the National Commission on Refugees (CONARE) were disbanded contras and their families.[35]

The prospect of thousands of former contras, disbanded without U.S. support, became an additional potential nightmare. Managing the effects of the U.S. contra war was bad enough; the fallout from a Central American peace accord could prove even worse. Philip L. Shepherd warned, in 1984, that it would be impossible to destabilize Nicaragua without also destabilizing Honduras. Every year that passed, the effects of militarization left more scars on Honduran life. As Shepherd put it:

The militarization of Honduras has become an end in itself, unrelated to any sensible U.S. foreign policy objectives. It has become a means not to peace, stability and development, but to the very conditions it was presumably designed to avoid: uncertainty, insecurity, instability, violence, repression and a loss of freedom and well-being.[36]

The questions remained: What was the alternative for Hondurans, given U.S. Central American policy? Would public opposition to the U.S. war move beyond mere protests into mass civil disobedience, strikes, or other kinds of active resistance? Then too, could mass popular opposition force the government to make changes, given the heavy Honduran indebtedness to the United States? By the late 1980s, it seemed, the possibilities of effective action for change remained severely limited.

13

The Way Ahead: A Conclusion

"Maybe Ronald Reagan has done us all a favour by bringing Hondurans together."

EFRAIN DIAZ ARRIVILLAGA, Christian Democrat Congressman

Growing opposition to the contra war seemed, by late 1987, to be producing that long-awaited spirit of nationalism. Whether this was something more than a convenient way to blame the outsider for national ills was yet to be seen. It was also debatable whether discontent would translate into enough pressure to achieve any concrete change. A history of failed hopes, and of bickering over responsibility for them, would provide stony ground for united commitment to new policies. But at least the energy for change was apparent.

Protests against the war grew louder and came from new quarters. At first, the presence of the contra and U.S. troops had not greatly affected the average Honduran. To protest against them was therefore more a political act than a defence of territory; besides, protesting was not a popular thing to do, because both forces were allegedly defending Honduras.

By 1986 both the contras and the U.S. troops were ubiquitous. The U.S. flag was burned in the streets, and the slogans that decorated city walls were not only anti-contra but also anti-United States. Demonstrations gathered as many as thirty thousand people in a city of half a million. It became dangerous for U.S. personnel to wander far from their barracks – or the brothels – and increasingly "correct" to speak against them.

Even the Nationalists chimed in. Rafael Leonardo Callejas, their leader, voiced the opinion that the contras were not wrong, but that they should be in Nicaragua not Honduras. Nationalist Nicolás Cruz Torres presented a wider motion to Congress against the contras, and joined other deputies in a mission to Washington to argue that the contras were a threat to Honduran democracy. The delegation told U.S. politicians that the contras were in Honduras against the will of the Honduran president and people, and were not capable of winning a war against the Sandinistas, anyway.[1] The businessmen who form the Nationalist Party base were becoming disenchanted, even those who had made money supplying the contras. There was gangland war over contra spoils, and many of the contra chiefs who did leave the country went without paying their bills.[2]

The politics of opposition to the contras, however, tended to have its self-serving side. For example, when Carlos Montoya, president of the National Congress and an aspiring candidate for the next elections, declared that the contra presence "heightens frictions with Nicaragua, but my country does not have the military capacity to expel them," he did this as part of a campaign to get more military and economic funds.[3] Montoya went to Europe in December 1986 and talked of alliances, including one with Japan, in preparation for what he called "an inevitable war with Nicaragua that is not of our part".[4] Such Nationalist criticism was therefore undoubtedly aimed at the U.S. Senate Foreign Relations Committee, which was holding up the sale of a dozen F-5E jets. President Azcona even travelled to Israel to talk about an alternative sale of Kfir jets, and diversification of Honduran interests led as far as the nation's first trade agreement with the Soviet Union.

The jets were important to Honduras in more than a strategic sense, because it was only in air power that the Honduran military had the advantage over a contra force with more men and better arms. The $100 million for the jets would have to come out of the total U.S. aid package, but fear of contra supremacy, not just national pride, made the deal desirable.

Fear of the contra presence in Honduras did not necessarily translate into approval of the Sandinistas. Anti-Sandinista propaganda had always been heavy; for example, *La Prensa* carried a regular insert called *Nicaragua Hoy* (Nicaragua Now), which promoted the contras as an alternative to Sandinista government. Posters produced by the right-wing Free Honduran Movement and speeches by armed forces chief Regalado about the "Communist menace next door" kept up the pressure. Proof of the success of such propaganda came in a Gallup poll taken in February 1986. While 80 per cent of those questioned saw conflicts along the border, or Nicaragua itself, as the principal problem afflicting their country, nearly 70 per cent also said that Honduras would be better off if the contras defeated the Sandinistas.[5] What was changing was attitudes to the contras and the U.S. military presence, because both of these forces were threatening the country's economy as well as its sovereignty.

Such was the message from a surprising new source, the university (UNAH), which had been under right-wing control for five years. Its rector, Oswaldo Soto Ramos, was a former colleague of General Alvarez. Nevertheless, the UNAH council published a unanimous protest on June 25, 1987, stating: "We are concerned about the presence of foreign troops, the external pressure on our monetary and fiscal policy and the presence of Nicaraguan counter-revolutionaries in Honduras, which compromises our neutrality."[6]

Protests affected and united the right wing and the left. There was bad news everywhere that hurt them both: the closing of Rosario Mining, which put twelve hundred miners out of work; the failure of Taiwanization (establishment of free zones and assembly plants); the increase in unemployment to an official 41 per cent. Azcona's solutions, including establishment of a stock exchange, raised more eyebrows than hopes within the business community while his budget cuts, including a 25 per cent slash in health spending, angered the populace.

Azcona takes the heat

Azcona's government had proved to be a "do-nothing" administration. Critics cited his vacillation, his subservience to the United States, lethargy in reform, lack of sympathy for displaced peasants, refusal to consult colleagues, and his tolerance of increasing repression. He was too obviously impotent. For example, he publicly refused contra leaders permission to hold meetings on Honduran soil, and then turned a blind eye to two such meetings the same week.[7]

Jaime Rosenthal, one of Azcona's presidential deputies, charged that the president had mismanaged his $5.5 million discretionary fund and that state enterprises were nests of corruption and inefficiency. The examples he gave included the Olancho Industrial Forestry Corporation (CORFINO) which had used up $400 million without exporting one cord of wood. There was the $100 million Henecan Harbor, impossible for boats to enter, and similar fiascos with palm oil and cashew projects. Allegations of corruption also alarmed the foreign aid community, so that the European Economic Community reduced its milk donations to schools from three thousand to one thousand tons because seven hundred tons had disappeared from a previous donation.[8]

When the labour movement seemed to be united against him, Azcona adopted the traditional ploy of encouraging division. For example, his close friend, Mario Espinal, head of the National Agrarian Institute (INA), set peasant groups against the INA union (SITRAINA) in May 1986, and one year later turned peasant groups against each other when another protest led to widespread land occupations. Azcona intervened personally, but refused to remove Espinal, who was able to negotiate separately with the National Union of Peasants (UNC) and thereby break a threatening alliance of all the peasant groups.[9]

The government's other response, repression, only alienated the nation more. Again, the peasant movement was at the heart of the crisis. On May 20, 1987, some hundred thousand peasants invaded thirty-five thousand acres of land in northwest Honduras, making perhaps the largest land invasion in Honduran history. The invasion forced the INA to process their claims, but the security police (FUSEP) arrested 450 peasants under the Alvarez anti-terrorism law of 1984. At least three peasants died in confrontations with police and the landowners banded together in the Honduran Farmers and Cattle Ranchers' Federation (FENAGH), the group responsible for peasant massacres in the 1970s.[10]

The rhetoric of repression soon sounded more like Alvarez than Alvarez himself. So an armed forces communiqué warned of "evil Hondurans" with "a terrorist plot to destabilize the government and to create confusion". It ended on a chilling note: "Hondurans, remember that in the defence of the Fatherland, we are all part of the Armed Forces."[11] As Dr. Ramón Custodio, president of the human rights organization CODEH, remarked, "All of a sudden everything is falling apart."[12]

A $20 million blackmail

The case of an obscure Puerto Rican rancher dramatized the Honduran debacle. Temístocles Ramírez, a U.S. citizen, had run a fourteen thousand-acre cattle ranch in northern Honduras through a Honduran company because, as a foreigner, he could not own land within twenty-five miles of the Atlantic coast. The local *Garífunas* (descendants of black slaves from the island of St. Vincent) disputed his ownership and lived on part of the land until it was expropriated in 1983 for construction of the Central American military school (CREM) intended for Salvadoran troops. Ramírez claimed $10 million reparation; the Honduran government is said to have offered him $3 million. He went to the U.S. Senate, which set the figure at $20 million and stated not only that Honduras owed it to him but also that it would have to come out of funds promised in aid. The note of May 7, 1987 read:

The State Department wishes to inform you that the U.S. Congress is ready to take action in the sense of suspending American aid, both economic and military, for the fiscal year 1988 to 1989 unless the government of Honduras realizes substantial progress in the determining of a just compensation to the claim of Mr. Temístocles Ramírez.[13]

On June 29 the U.S. Congress announced that it would hold back $20 million of a promised $60 million until compensation was agreed upon. The decision infuriated Honduran Congressmen, who passed a resolution demanding that no money be paid unless agreed upon by a Honduran court or an international tribunal. It was, they said, a fine example of the popular saying: "The devil pays poorly those who serve him best."[14]

The case also incensed the *Garífunas* who disputed Ramírez's ownership. For the first time, the black minorities of Honduras began to join protests. The nearly thirty thousand *Miskito* Hondurans were also voicing their own discontent, partly in response to a Honduran military crackdown in their border area, and partly to news of the autonomy being offered to Nicaraguan *Miskitos* by the Sandinista government. Without a single high school or hospital, Honduran *Miskitos* were feeling ignored, and beginning to express their resentment.[15]

The U.S. war in Central America was stirring up new discontent. But could someone else's war translate into a united movement for change? Or would the Honduran government continue, as the old saying goes, to have opponents but not opposition?

Opposition or opportunism?

The Nationalist opposition must be measured against its fundamental interests – those of big business, most of which are U.S. owned. Callejas himself, a graduate of Mississippi University, had not yet spoken a word against the Reagan administration, only against the contra presence in Honduras. Indeed, Callejas sometimes seemed more American than Honduran, especially in the style of his $3 million election campaign, which emphasized a youthful, slick image, and adopted the high-tech hustle of U.S. electoral campaigning rather than the folksiness of traditional Honduran politicking.

Little change could be expected from within the Liberal Party. The Reina brothers, Carlos Roberto and Jorge Antonio, of ALIPO (Popular Liberal Alliance) and then M-LIDER (the Liberal Democratic Revolutionary Movement, a reformist wing of the Liberal Party), had left to form their own Socialist Party. It seemed unrealistic to expect immediate mass support either for that party or for the Democratic Action Party formed in 1987 by former armed forces chief Wálter López, given the reluctance of most voters to go beyond the traditional two parties. The Christian Democrats (PDCH) were still split into two wings. The PDCH was outside the framework of the mainstream Christian Democrat parties of Latin America, which gave it independence but also limited international support. Nor was there evidence of the mass protest movement producing many converts to the even smaller left-wing parties before the next presidential elections slated for the end of 1989.

More could be expected from the growing coalescence of the labour movement around sovereignty issues and social reform. However, a Honduran worker's demand for a decent wage or a peasant's demand for land was not easily translated into a wider political sphere of action. Against the objective conditions for discontent must be set the subjective conditions of Honduran society.

Many students of Honduran society have commented on Honduran moderation, on the mitigating influence of relative freedom of the press and an active labour movement. There is also the psychological character of Hondurans, much romanticized by foreigners as innocence. It might more accurately be seen as sound common sense: "The Honduran people are not romantics. They don't go for fine rhetoric, but for practical goals – a roof, a job, some beans to eat. They are not fooled by promises or easily inspired to risk losing what little they have."[16]

Hondurans seemed unlikely, then, to opt for revolution. Their patience enabled them to outlast disasters and, in general, to avoid the worst excesses of totalitarian rule that have afflicted their neighbours. The usual compromises have so far enabled life to go on, until faced with a Central American conflict where muddling through hardly seems a solution. Optimists point out that events in Honduras never quite happen as expected, that the least-promising presidents have turned out to be not so bad after all, and that, somehow, Hondurans have survived what statistics show as disaster after disaster. Others point out that the miseries of such survival – the malnutrition, disease, unemployment, lack of water or proper housing – are all worse in Honduras than in even war-torn El Salvador, in Guatemala, or in Nicaragua.

Like its neighbours, Honduras could show no real improvement while enlisted in the U.S. Central American war. And the nation's ability to influence that war had been severely curtailed by its dependence on the United States. Diplomatically, it had become a very minor actor, despite its strategic importance.

While José Napoleón Duarte of El Salvador seemed to have the White House ear, and Vinicio Cerezo of Guatemala proclaimed neutrality for his own purposes, Azcona was reduced to a "me too" position, tagging on the heels of Duarte. So Azcona helped Duarte to scuttle plans for the first June 1987 meeting of Central American premiers, in the interests of the United States. And, when all nations finally came to an agreement, primarily to keep the United States from imposing its own anti-Sandinista plan, Honduras was merely a silent partner.

Honduras had never been a supporter of the Contadora group's peaceful solution to the conflict. Its contra complicity led Nicaragua to take Honduras to the World Court in 1986. Although Nicaragua agreed to drop the suit in the interests of the Guatemala City Peace Accord, relations did not noticeably improve.

The effects of the contra war were indeed ironic. The Nicaragua suit at the World Court held up the Honduran suit against its old enemy, El Salvador, over border issues dating back to the 1969 Soccer War. Honduras had not been able to settle one war with a neighbour before becoming imbroiled in another. The contra war also got in the way of Honduras's most prized new export – electricity. Power from the El Cajón dam was sold to Costa Rica and Nicaragua, at least until the contras kept cutting power lines.

Alienated by past history from El Salvador and by its U.S. bargain from Nicaragua, Honduras had also cut relations with its northern neighbour, Guatemala, primarily because of disputes over trade.

The historic economic isolation, increased by Central American Common Market inequities, had now extended to a more general seclusion. Ironically, the nation of Morazán, champion of Central American unity, had become isolated from its neighbours, and from both the political left and right. If Honduras had indeed become "the centre of the universe" for one U.S. soldier, few would agree with him – probably not even fellow Marines.

Jumping ship

Jumping overboard from the USS Honduras is not a likely course of action given the present scenario. The National Party may have criticized Liberal subservience to the United States while it was out of power, but seemed even less likely than the Liberals to pick a fight with Washington if it became a government. What seemed most likely in mainstream Honduran politics was the building of a movement to pressure for better U.S. terms, to restore a little autonomy without jeopardizing the U.S. funding that has always depended on U.S. interests rather than client servility. Attracting aid and investment from other private or foreign government sources would be possible only with peace in the region. By lending its territory to war, Honduras was preventing itself from enjoying any of the rewards of peace.

Obviously, Nicaragua was the nation with the most to gain from cessation of the U.S. contra war. Peace was the first need, but it could not, alone, produce the social or economic justice for which the Sandinistas, the Farabundo Martí Liberation Front in El Salvador, or the National Revolutionary Unity of Guatemala had been fighting. Honduras, too, would have to do more than quit the U.S. ranks if it was to find any measure of social prosperity. It would have to implement fundamental change.

In such a traditional, isolated, and divided society, with such a long history of exploitation and chaos and so short an experience of genuine development or public will, the way ahead was likely to prove as rocky as the roads of the Honduran past.

List of Acronyms

ACASCH
Asociación Campesina Social-Cristiana de Honduras
Social-Christian Peasant Association of Honduras

AFL-CIO
American Federation of Labour / Congress of Industrial Organizations

AID
Agency for International Development

AIFLD
American Institute for Free Labour Development

ANACH
Asociación Nacional de Campesinos Hondureños
National Association of Honduran Peasants

APROCAFE
Asociación de Productores de Café
Association of Coffee Producers

APROH
Asociación para el Progreso de Honduras
Association for Honduran Progress

CACM
Central American Common Market

CAUSA
Confederation of Associations for the Unity of American Societies

CCOP
Comité Coordinadora de las Organizaciónes Populares
Co-ordinating Committee of Popular Organizations

CEDOH
Centro de Documentación de Honduras
Honduran Centre of Documentation

CELAM
Conferencia Episcopal de América Latina
Latin American Bishops' Conference

CGT
Central General de Trabajadores
General Congress of Workers

CODEH
Comité para la Defensa de Derechos Humanos de Honduras
Committee for the Defence of Human Rights in Honduras

COFADEH
Comité de las Familias de los Detenidos y Desaparecidos Hondureños
Committee of the Families of the Detained and Disappeared of Honduras

COLPROSUMAH
Colegio Profesional Superior Magisterial Hondureño
Honduran College of Teachers in Higher Education

CONADI
Corporación Nacional de Inversiones
State Investment Corporation

CONCORDE
Consejo Coordinador de Desarrollo
Co-ordinating Council for Development

CONDECA
Consejo de la Defensa de Centroamérica
Central American Defence Council

CONOCH
Consejo Nacional de Obreros y Campesinos de Honduras
National Council of Workers and Peasants of Honduras

COSUFA
Consejo Superior de las Fuerzas Armadas
Armed Forces' Superior Council

CTH
Confederación de Trabajadores de Honduras
Confederation of Honduran Workers

FDR / FMLN
Frente Democrático Revolucionario / Frente Farabundo Martí para la
Liberación Nacional
Democratic Revolutionary Front / Farabundo Martí Front for National
Liberation

FECESITLIH
Federación Central de Sindicatos Libres Hondureños
Central Federation of Honduran Free Trade Unions

FECORAH
Federación de Cooperativas de la Reforma Agraria
Federation of Agrarian Reform Co-operatives

FENACH
Federación Nacional de Campesinos Hondureños
National Federation of Honduran Peasants

FENAGH
Federación Nacional de Agricultores y Ganaderos de Honduras
National Federation of Honduran Cattlemen and Farmers

FMLNH
Frente Morazanista de Liberación Nacional de Honduras
Morazanist Liberation Front (Honduras)

FPH
Frente Patriótico Hondureño
Honduran Patriotic Front

FPR
Fuerzas Populares Revolucionarias "Lorenzo Zelaya"
Popular Revolutionary Forces (Lorenzo Zelaya)

FRU
Fuerzas Revolutionarias Universitarias
Revolutionary University Forces

FSH
Federación Sindical Hondureña
Honduran Union Federation

FUNACAMH
Frente de Unidad Nacional de Campesinos Hondureños
National Unity Front of Honduran Peasants

FUNC
Frente de Unidad Campesina
Front of Campesino Unity

FUSEP
Fuerzas de Seguridad Pública
Public Security Forces

FUTH
Federación Unitaria de Trabajadores Hondureños
United Federation of Honduran Workers

FUUD
Frente Unido Universitario para la Democracia
United University Democratic Front

IMF
International Monetary Fund

INA
Instituto Nacional Agrario
National Agrarian Institute

MPL
Movimiento Popular de Liberación "Cinchoneros"
Popular Liberation Movement "Cinchoneros"

OAS
Organization of American States

ORIT
Inter-American Regional Organization of Labour

PCH-ML
Partido Comunista Hondureño Marxista-Leninista
Honduran Communist Party (Marxist-Leninist)

PDCH
Partido Demócráta Cristiano de Honduras
Christian Democrat Party of Honduras

PINU
Partido de Innovación y Unidad
Innovation and Unity Party

PRTC-H
Partido Revolucionario de los Trabajadores Centroamericanos
Revolutionary Party of Central American Workers

SITRASFRUCO
Sindicato de Trabajadores de Standard Fruit Company
Standard Fruit Company Workers' Union

SITRATERCO
Sindicato de Trabajadores de la Tela Railroad Company
Tela Railroad Company Workers' Union

STENEE
Sindicato de Trabajadores de la Empresa Nacional de Energia Electria
Union of National Electric Company Workers

HONDURAS

TACA
Transportes Aereos de Centro América
Central American Air Transport

UNAH
Universidad Nacional Autonoma Hondureña
National Autonomous University of Honduras

UNC
Unión Nacional de Campesinos
National Union of Peasants

UNHCR
United Nations' High Commission for Refugees

Notes

Full details on sources are given in Bibliography.

CHAPTER 1 An Introduction

1 The most thorough Honduran study in English was published in 1950: S.W. Stokes, *Honduras: An Area Study in Government.* I have made extensive use of Longino Becerra's *Evolución Histórica de Honduras,* 1983, a storehouse of historical comments on the Honduran past. *Honduras: Portrait of a Captive Nation,* 1985, edited by Nancy Peckenham and Annie Street, usefully compiles and translates Honduran comment and analysis.

2 Thomas P. Anderson, *Politics in Central America,* p. 136.

3 Jack Epstein, *Along the Gringo Trail,* p. 131.

4 *New York Review of Books,* March 27, 1986.

5 Alex Abella, *The Total Banana,* p. 172.

6 *Los Angeles Times,* December 4, 1982.

7 Honduran Chancellor Cesar A. Batres at the United Nations, quoted by Becerra, p. 205.

8 Becerra, p. 34.

9 Linda Nelson, *The Cost of Conquest: Indian Decline in Honduras Under Spanish Rule,* p. 33.

10 *Worldmark Encyclopedia of the Nations:* 1987.

11 William H. Durham, *Scarcity and Survival in Central America,* p. 107.

CHAPTER 2 Through Foreign Eyes

1 Ariel Dorfman, *How to Read Donald Duck,* p. 75.

2 Ibid.

3 Robert W. Desmond, *The Press and World Affairs,* p. 372.

4 Frantz Fanon, *Black Skin, White Masks,* p. 18.

5 C. Wright Mills, *Power, Politics and People,* p. 405.

6 For this analysis I am indebted to Edward Said's study of press coverage of Middle East affairs, in Edward W. Said, *Covering Islam,* p. 27.

7 Quoted in R.S. Chamberlain, *The Conquest and Colonization of Honduras, 1502 to 1550,* p. 3.

8 Franklin Parker, *The Central American Republics,* p. 2.

9 *El Tiempo,* Nov. 17, 1984.

10 J.L. Stephens, *Incidents of Travel in Central America, Chiapas and Yucatan,* p. 212.

11 Quoted in Francis Robicsek, *Copán, Home of the Mayan Gods,* p. 29.

12 O. Henry, *Cabbages and Kings,* p. V.

13 Ibid., p. 145.

14 Richard Harding Davis, *Adventures and Letters,* p. 143.

15 Ibid., p. 145.

16 Richard Harding Davis, *Three Gringos in Venezuela and Central America,* p. 147.

17 Quoted in Gordon Connell-Smith, *The United States and Latin America,* p. 115.

18 Quoted in Jenny Pearce, *Under the Eagle,* p. 20.

19 John Dos Passos, *The 42nd Parallel,* p. 236.

20 Louis Sheaffer, *O'Neill,* p. 152.

21 Ibid., p. 54.

22 Harry A. Franck, *Tramping Through Mexico, Guatemala and Honduras,* p. 328.

23 Aldous Huxley, *Beyond the Mexique Bay,* p. 207.

24 Paul Theroux, *The Mosquito Coast,* p. 102.

25 Ibid., p. 109.

26 Abella, p. 33.

27 Ibid., p. 176.

28 Ibid., p. 120.

29 The Editors of Life and Rand McNally, *Life Pictorial Atlas of the World,* 1961, p. 229.

30 William Krehm, *Democracies and Tyrannies of the Caribbean,* p. 79.

31 *El Tiempo,* Nov. 17, 1984.

CHAPTER 3 The Spanish Empire

1 Becerra, p. 23. The quote at the beginning of the chapter is also from Becerra, p. 62.

2 Quoted in Becerra, p. 44.

3 Quoted in Becerra, p. 44.

4 *C.I.A. World Fact Book,* 1986.

5 Benjamin Keen, *A Short History of Latin America,* p. 5.

6 Quoted in Becerra, p. 57.

7 Becerra, p. 56.

8 Quoted in Becerra, p. 54.
9 Quoted in Becerra, p. 57.
10 Quoted in Becerra, p. 56.
11 Quoted in Becerra, p. 55.
12 Stokes, p. 30.
13 Keen, p. 74.
14 Quoted in Becerra, p. 65.
15 Becerra, p. 66.
16 Quoted in Becerra, p. 67.
17 Quoted in Becerra, p. 64.
18 Becerra, p. 63.
19 Murdo J. MacLeod, *Spanish Central America*, p. 120.
20 Ralph Woodward, Jr., *Central America: A Nation Divided*, p. 45.
21 Stokes, p. 31.
22 MacLeod, p. 202.
23 Parker, p. 47.
24 Becerra, p. 123.
25 Rafael Heliodoro Valle, *Historia de la Cultura Hondureña*, p. 123.

CHAPTER 4 Independence and Civil War

1 Keen, p. 102; and Woodward, p. 79.
2 Woodward, p. 57.
3 Keen, p. 145.
4 Quoted in Becerra, p. 79.
5 Ibid., p. 78.
6 Quoted in Becerra, p. 81.
7 Becerra, p. 85.
8 Quoted in Becerra, p. 86.
9 Becerra, p. 89.
10 Parker, p. 79.
11 Woodward, p. 91.
12 Rafael Montúfar, *Francisco Morazán*, p. 88.
13 See, for instance, Thomas L. Karnes, *The Failure of Union*, p. 69; Montúfar, p. 58; and Woodward, p. 104.
14 Woodward, p. 103.
15 Stephens, p. 249.
16 Mario Rodríguez, *Central America*, p. 72.
17 Quoted in Thomas L. Karnes, *The Failure of Union: Central America 1824-1875*, p. 88.
18 Harry K. Meyer, *Historical Dictionary of Honduras*, p. 242.

19 Karnes, p. 92.

CHAPTER 5 The Age of Adventurism

1 Quoted in Antonio Murga Frassinetti, *Enclave y Sociedad en Honduras*, p. 15.
2 Quoted in Mario Rodríguez, *A Palmerstonian Diplomat in Central America: Frederick Chatfield*, p. 237.
3 Quoted in Rodríguez, *Palmerstonian Diplomat*, p. 121.
4 Quoted in Rodríquez, *Palmerstonian Diplomat*, p. 219.
5 Quoted in Connell-Smith, p. 62.
6 Gordon H. Stuart, *Latin America and the United States*, p. 49.
7 Becerra, p. 111.
8 Pablo Neruda, "The United Fruit Company," *Collected Poems*.
9 Quoted in Connell-Smith, p. 4.
10 Quoted in Rodríguez, *Palmerstonian Diplomat*, p. 295.
11 Quoted in Norman Graebner, *The Monroe Doctrine*, p. 320.
12 Quoted in Stuart, p. 302.
13 Rodríguez, *Central America*, p. 93.
14 María Soltera, *A Lady's Ride Across Honduras*, p. XII.

CHAPTER 6 The Banana Empires

1 Quoted in Murga, p. 61.
2 Krehm, p. 81.
3 See, for instance, Juan Arancibia, *Honduras: un Estado Nacional?*, p. 29.
4 Murga. p. 43.
5 Quoted in Becerra, p. 128.
6 Quoted in Murga, p. 42.
7 Stephen Schlesinger and Stephen Kinzer, *Bitter Fruit*, p. 66.
8 Becerra, p. 147.
9 Richard Lapper, *Honduras: State for Sale*, p. 31.
10 Ramón Amaya Amador, *Prisión Verde*, p. 17.
11 Becerra, p. 147.
12 Richard Burbach and Patricia Flynn, *Agribusiness in the Americas*, p. 15.
13 Murga, p. 101.
14 Tom Barry, Beth Wood and Deb Preusch, *Dollars and Dictators*, p. 19.
15 See Mario Ribas, "A Central American Indictment of the United States," in Nancy Peckenham and Annie Street (eds.), *Honduras: Portrait of a Captive Nation*, p. 58.
16 See the report by Dana G. Munro, head of the U.S. legation in Nicaragua, in Peckenham and Street, p. 69.
17 Krehm, p. 84.
18 Ibid., p. 87.

19 Quoted in Becerra, p. 149.
20 Schlesinger and Kinzer, p. 86.
21 Krehm, p. 88.
22 Stephen Volk, "Honduras: On the Border of War," in *NACLA Report on the Americas*, Nov.-Dec. 1981, p. 8.
23 Tom Barry and Deb Preusch, *The Central American Fact Book*, p. 150.
24 Ibid., p. 152.
25 Ibid., p. 265.
26 Woodward, p. 186.

CHAPTER 7 Party Politics

1 Gregorio Selser, in Introduction to Krehm, p. VII.
2 Arancibia, p. 45.
3 Quoted in E. Bradford Burns, *The Poverty of Progress*, p. 92.
4 Quoted in Burns, p. 92.
5 Quoted in James W. Gantenbern, *Evolution of Our Latin American Policy*, p. 74.
6 The discussion of conservatism and liberalism following is from Ralph J. Woodward Jr., "The Rise and Decline of Liberalism in Central America," in *Journal of Inter-American Studies*, Vol. 26, No. 3, August 1986.
7 Burns, p. 55.
8 Stokes, p. 208.
9 Ibid., p. 189.
10 Ibid., p. 239.
11 CEDOH, *Boletín Informativo*, March 1986, p. 10.
12 Edward R.F. Sheehan, "The Country of Nada," in *New York Review of Books*, March 27, 1986, p. 13.
13 Mark B. Rosenberg, in Introduction to Mark Rosenberg and L. Shepherd (eds.), *Honduras Confronts Its Future: Contending Perspectives on Critical Issues*, p. 7.
14 Krehm, p. 91.
15 Ibid.
16 Washington Office on Latin America, *Honduran Elections and Democracy: Withered by Washington*, February 1986.
17 Elvia Alvarado, *Don't Be Afraid, Gringo: A Honduran Woman Speaks from the Heart*, p. 106.
18 Ibid.

CHAPTER 8 The Rise of Labour

1 Victor Meza, *Historia del Movimiento Obrero Hondureño*, p. 4.
2 Becerra, p. 151.
3 Meza, p. 11.

4 Quoted in Meza, p. 13.

5 Becerra, p. 153.

6 Meza, p. 208.

7 Lapper, p. 31.

8 Quoted in David Kepner, *Social Aspects of the Banana Industry*, p. 160.

9 Amaya Amador, p. 133.

10 Meza, p. 19.

11 Ibid., p. 52.

12 See Tom Barry and Deb Preusch, *AIFLD in Central America: Agents as Organizers*.

13 Meza, p. 90.

14 Quoted in Lapper, p. 38.

15 Quoted in Meza, p. 100.

16 Lapper, p. 39.

17 Becerra, p. 154.

18 Quoted in Richard Swedberg, "From Legalization to Repression: The Labour Movement After 1954," in Peckenham and Street, p. 104.

19 Lapper, p. 40.

20 Robert MacCameron, *Bananas, Labor and Politics in Honduras*, p. 99.

21 Lapper, p. 40.

22 Quoted in Meza, p. 127.

23 Quoted in Pedro Antonio Brizuela, "Testimony of a Workers' Leader," in Peckenham and Street, p. 117.

24 *Honduras Update*, April 1985.

25 CEDOH, *Boletín Informativo*, August 1986.

26 Lapper, p. 11.

27 Colegio Hondureño de Economistas, quoted in *Latin American Regional Report*, Oct. 30, 1986.

CHAPTER 9 Peasants and Priests

1 Durham, p. 22.

2 Padre J. Guadalupe Carney, *To Be a Revolutionary*, p. 280.

3 Lapper, p. 49.

4 Barry and Preusch, *Central American Fact Book*, p. 253.

5 Quoted in Douglas Kincaid, "'We Are the Agrarian Reform': Rural Politics and Agrarian Reform," in Peckenham and Street, p. 136.

6 Lapper, p. 52.

7 Douglas Kincaid, "'We Are the Agrarian Reform'," in *Mesoamérica*, May-October 1983.

8 *Honduras Update*, March 1985.

9 Kincaid, "'We Are the Agrarian Reform'," in Peckenham and Street, p. 138.

10 Durham, p. 35.
11 Ibid., p. 108.
12 Ibid., p. 162.
13 Mario Posas, *El Movimiento Campesino Hondureño*, p. 27.
14 Lapper, p. 67.
15 Kincaid, "'We Are the Agrarian Reform'," in Peckenham and Street, p. 146.
16 Lapper, p. 80.
17 Philip Shepherd, "Wisconsin in Honduras: Agrarian Politics and U.S. Influence in the 1980s," in Peckenham and Street, p. 159.
18 *Honduras Update*, July 1985.
19 Shepherd, "Wisconsin in Honduras," in Peckenham and Street, p. 161.
20 Ibid., p. 163.
21 Interview with author, Las Milpas, Honduras, 1984.
22 *Honduras Update*, June/July 1987.
23 Peckenham and Street, p. 168.
24 Quoted in Penny Lernoux, *Cry of the People*, p. 391.
25 Quoted in Becerra, p. 198.
26 Lernoux, p. 114.
27 Quoted in Lernoux, p. 123.
28 *Honduras Update*, March 1984.
29 Carney, p. 197.
30 Americas Watch, *Human Rights in Honduras: Central America's Sideshow.*
31 *La Prensa*, Nov. 11, 1983.
32 *El Tiempo*, August 21, 1986.
33 CEDOH, *Boletín Informativo*, No. 23, March 1983.
34 CEDOH, *Boletín Informativo*, No. 21, February 1983.
35 CEDOH, *Boletín Informativo*, No. 23, March 1983.
36 *La Tribuna*, June 26, 1986.

CHAPTER 10 The People Speak

1 Daniel Camacho and Rafael Menjivar, *Movimientos Populares en América Central*, pp. 250, 266.
2 *New York Times*, March 9, 1987.
3 CEDOH, *Boletín Informativo*, March 1987.
4 Alan Fajardo Reina, in *Pensamiento Propio*, No. 38, reprinted in *Honduras Update*, April 1987.
5 Americas Watch, p. 12.
6 Honduran Human Rights Commission, *Report*, 1986.
7 *Honduras Briefing*, March 1987.
8 *Americas Watch Bulletin*, January 1988.

9 *Miami Herald,* Nov. 17, 1986.

10 *Honduras Update,* August 1987.

11 Americas Watch, p. 111.

12 Ibid., p. 2.

13 Becerra, p. 152.

14 Annie Street, "Worker Co-ops in Honduras," in Women's International Resource Exchange, *Honduran Women: The Marginalized Majority,* p. 13.

15 Krehm, p. 99.

16 Nancy Peckenham and Annie Street, "Women: Honduras's Marginalized Majority," in Peckenham and Street, p. 234.

17 Ibid., p. 233.

18 Quoted in Peckenham and Street, "Women," p. 234.

19 Peckenham and Street, "Women," p. 234.

20 Interview with author, Tegucigalpa, Honduras, 1984.

21 Quoted in *Honduras Update,* May 1987.

22 Ibid.

23 Peckenham and Street, p. 267.

24 *Food First Alert,* 1987.

CHAPTER 11 The Military Connection

1 MacCameron, p. 136.

2 Steve C. Ropp, "The Honduran Army in the Sociopolitical Evolution of Honduras," in *The Americas,* Vol. XXX, April 1974, p. 504.

3 Ibid., p. 507.

4 Krehm, p. 94.

5 Barry and Preusch, *Central America Fact Book,* p. 121.

6 Schlesinger and Kinzer, p. 219.

7 Quoted in James Morris, *Honduras: Caudillo Politics and Military Rulers,* p. 12.

8 Ropp, p. 523.

9 MacCameron, p. 97.

10 Peckenham and Street, p. 275.

11 Becerra, p. 172.

12 Pearce, p. 60.

13 Quoted in Pearce, p. 60.

14 Durham, p. 16.

15 Quoted in Becerra, p. 189.

16 U.S. Department of State Congressional Presentation, *Security Assistance Programs 1981-1983,* cited in Richard Alan White, *The Morass,* p. 183.

17 *Washington Post,* March 28, 1980.

18 CEDOH, *Los Refugiados Salvadoreños en Honduras,* 1982, pp. 19-22.X.

19 Washington Office on Latin America and Epica Task Force, quoted in Lapper, p. 80.
20 Quoted in Lapper, p. 80.
21 *El Día*, Nov. 21, 1983.
22 *Inforpress Centroamericano*, No. 520, Nov. 25, 1982.
23 *Newsweek*, Nov. 8, 1982.
24 *The Tower Commission Report*, p. 466.
25 *Washington Post*, May 26, 1984.
26 Americas Watch, p. 117.
27 *Honduras Update*, January 1987.
28 CEDOH, *Boletín Informativo*, May 1987.
29 Quoted in Alan Nairn, "The United States Militarizes Honduras," in Peckenham and Street, p. 297.
30 *The Tower Commission Report*, p. 458.
31 Full details of the Israeli supplies are listed in Jonathan Marshall, Peter Dale Scott and Jane Hunter, *The Iran-Contra Connection*, pp. 115-118.
32 Americas Watch, p. 10.

CHAPTER 12 Losing Out in the U.S. War Games

1 Philip L. Shepherd, "The Tragic Causes and Consequences of U.S. Policy in Honduras," *World Policy Review*, Vol. II, No. 1, Fall 1984.
2 "Honduras: An International Dialogue," a conference held in Miami, November 1984, reported in Rosenberg and Shepherd.
3 *El Tiempo*, March 31, 1985.
4 *El Tiempo*, Feb. 29, 1985.
5 CEDOH, *Boletín Informativo*, October 1984.
6 Ibid.
7 *Honduras Update*, February 1985.
8 Testimony to CODEH, 1987.
9 Americas Watch, pp. 126-142.
10 Wálter López, interviewed on "Sixty Minutes," CBS-TV, March 29, 1987.
11 CEDOH, *Boletín Informativo*, March 1987.
12 Department of State Bulletin, August 1984.
13 *El Tiempo*, Dec. 1, 1981.
14 *La Tribuna*, June 27, 1983.
15 Lapper, p. 98.
16 *New York Times*, April 1, 1985.
17 *Central America Report*, Feb. 13, 1987.
18 *Newsweek*, April 14, 1986.
19 *El Tiempo*, March 31, 1987.

20 *The Globe and Mail* (Toronto), March 29, 1988, p. 1.
21 *Newsday* interview, published in *Washington Post,* August 25, 1986.
22 "Sixty Minutes," CBS-TV, March 29, 1987.
23 CEDOH, *Boletín Informativo,* June 1987.
24 Ibid., September 1984.
25 Quoted in *Central America Report,* Jan. 3, 1987.
26 *El Tiempo,* Sept. 14, 1984.
27 *El Tiempo,* May 28 and May 30, 1984.
28 *New York Times,* Feb. 7, 1984.
29 Quoted in *Mesoamérica,* May 1986.
30 *El Tiempo,* June 2, 1986.
31 CEDOH, *Boletín Informativo,* June 1987.
32 "Morning Edition," National Public Radio, April 11, 1984.
33 *Mesoamérica,* June 1987.
34 *El Tiempo,* July 14, 1987.
35 CEDOH, *Boletín Informativo,* July 1987.
36 Philip Shepherd, in *World Policy Journal,* Fall 1984, p. 148.

CHAPTER 13 The Way Ahead: A Conclusion

1 *El Tiempo,* April 30, 1987.
2 *El Tiempo,* June 1, 1987.
3 *La Prensa,* Jan. 30, 1987.
4 *La Tribuna,* Dec. 26, 1986.
5 *Mesoamérica,* May 1986.
6 CEDOH, *Boletín Informativo,* July 1987.
7 *Central American Report,* June 26, 1987.
8 *Central American Report,* May 15, 1987.
9 *Honduras Update,* June/July 1987.
10 *Central American Report,* June 26, 1987.
11 *Honduras Update,* August 1987.
12 Ibid.
13 Ibid.
14 CEDOH, *Boletín Informativo,* July 1987.
15 *Washington Post,* June 11, 1987.
16 Victor Meza, personal interview, Tegucigalpa, Honduras, 1984.

Bibliography

1 Books

Abella, Alex, *The Total Banana*, New York and London: Harcourt Brace, 1978.

Alba, Victor, *Nationalists Without Nations*, New York: Praeger, 1968.

Alvarado, Elvia, *Don't Be Afraid, Gringo: A Honduran Woman Speaks from the Heart*, San Francisco: Food First Books, 1987.

Amaya Amador, Ramón, *Prisión Verde*, Tegucigalpa: Baktun, 1950.

Americas Watch, *Human Rights in Honduras: Central America's Sideshow*, New York and Washington: Americas Watch Press, 1987.

Anderson, Thomas, P., *Politics in Central America: Guatemala, El Salvador, Honduras and Nicaragua*, New York: Praeger, 1982.

———, "Honduras in Transition", *Current History*, March 1985.

Arancibia, Juan, *Honduras: Un Estado Nacional?* Tegucigalpa: Guaymuras, 1981.

Argueta, Mario y Edgardo Quiñónez, *Historia de Honduras*, Tegucigalpa: Escuela Superior, 1978.

Asturias, Miguel Angel, *The Green Pope*, New York: Delacorte, 1971.

Bancroft, Hubert Howe, *History of Central America*, San Francisco: The History Company, 1887.

Barry, Tom and Deb Preusch, *AIFLD in Central America: Agents as Organizers*, Albuquerque: The Resource Centre, 1986.

———, *Central America Fact Book*, Albuquerque: The Resource Centre, 1986.

Barry, Tom, Beth Wood and Deb Preusch, *Dollars & Dictators*, Albuquerque: The Resource Centre, 1982.

Becerra, Longino, *Evolución Histórica de Honduras*, Tegucigalpa: Baktun, 1983.

Beale, Carleton, *Banana Gold*, London and Philadelphia: Lippincott, 1932.

Buckley, Tom, *Violent Neighbors*, New York: Times Books, 1984.

Burbach, Roger and Patricia Flynn, *Agribusiness in the Americas*, New York: Monthly Review Press, 1980.

Burns, E. Bradford, *The Poverty of Progress: Latin America in the Nineteenth Century*, Berkeley: University of California Press, 1980.

Camacho, Daniel and Rafael Menjivar, *Movimientos Populares en Centroamérica*, San José: EDUCA, 1985.

Camacho, Daniel and Manuel Rojas, *La Crisis Centroamericana*, San José: FLACSO, 1984.

Carney, James, *To Be a Revolutionary*, San Francisco: Harper & Row, 1985.

Chamberlain, R.S., *The Conquest and Colonization of Honduras, 1502 to 1550*, Washington: Carnegie Institute, 1953.

Chechi, Vincent, *Honduras, A Problem of Economic Development*, New York: Twentieth Century Fund Press, 1959.

Connell-Smith, Gordon, *The United States and Latin America*, London: Heinemann, 1974.

Consejo Superior Universitario Centroamericano, *El Universo Bananero en Centroamérica*, San José: EDUCA, 1977.

Davis, Richard Harding, *Adventures and Letters*, New York: Scribner's, 1917.

———, *Three Gringos in Venezuela and Central America*, New York: Harper, 1896.

Deskin, Martin, ed., *Trouble in Our Backyard*, New York: Pantheon, 1983.

Desmond, Linda, "The Indian Population of Colonial Honduras", *Mesoamérica* No. 9, January 1985.

Desmond, Robert W., *The Press and World Affairs*, New York: Arne, 1976.

Dorfman, Ariel, *How to Read Donald Duck*, New York: International General Press, 1975.

Dos Passos, John, *The 42nd Parallel*, New York: Houghton Mifflin, 1964.

Durham, William H., *Scarcity and Survival in Central America: Ecological Origins of the Soccer War*, Stanford: Stanford Press, 1979.

Durón, Rómulo, *Bosquejo Histórico de Honduras*, Tegucigalpa: Baktun, 1982.

Edward, Mike, "Honduras: Eye of the Storm," *National Geographic*, November 1983.

Epstein, Jack, *Along the Gringo Trail*, Berkeley: And / Or Press, 1977.

Etchison, Don L., *The United States and Militarism in Central America*, New York: Praeger, 1975.

Fanon, Frantz, *Black Skin, White Masks*, New York: Grove Press, 1967.

Fiallos, Carmen, *Conozca Honduras*, Tegucigalpa: Sec. de Cultura y Turismo, 1984.

Fields, Troy S., *Mosquitia*, Albuquerque: University of New Mexico Press, 1967.

Fonseca, Gautamo, *Cuatro Ensayos Sobre la Realidad Política de Honduras*, Tegucigalpa: Editorial Universitaria, 1980.

Franck, Harry A., *Tramping through Mexico, Guatemala and Honduras*, London: Fisher Unwin, 1916.

Funes de Torres, Lucinda, *Derechos Humanos en Honduras*, Tegucigalpa: CEDOH, 1984.

Galeano, Eduardo, *Open Veins of Latin America*, New York: Monthly Review Press, 1977.

Gantenbern, James W., *Evolution of Our Latin American Policy*, New York: Octagon, 1971.

Gerassi, John, *The Great Fear in Latin America*, New York: Macmillan, 1963.

Graebner, Norman, ed., *Manifest Destiny*, Indianapolis: Bobbs-Merrill, 1968.

Henry, O., *Cabbages and Kings*, New York: Doubleday, 1904.

Huxley, Aldous, *Beyond the Mexique Bay*, London: Chatto & Windus, 1934.

Karnes, Thomas L., *The Failure of Union: Central America 1824-1875*, Chapel Hill: University of North Carolina Press, 1961.

Keen, Benjamin, *A Short History of Latin America*, Boston: Houghton Mifflin, 1980.

———, *Readings in Latin America*, Boston: Houghton Mifflin, 1955.

Kelajarvi, Thorsten V., *Central America: Land of Lords and Lizards*, Princeton: Van Nostrand, 1962.

Kepner, C.D. and J.H. Soothill, *The Banana Empire: A Case Study in Economic Imperialism*, New York: Russell & Russell, 1967.

Keppner, C.D., *Social Aspects of the Banana Industry*, New York: Columbia University Press, 1936.

Kincaid, Douglas, "We Are the Agrarian Reform," *Mesoamérica*, May / October, 1983.

Krehm, William, *Democracies and Tyrannies of the Caribbean*, Westport: Lawrence Hill, 1984.

Langley, Lester, *Central America: The Real Stakes*, New York: Crown, 1985.

Lapper, Richard, *Honduras: State for Sale*, London: Latin American Bureau, 1985.

Lernoux, Penny, *Cry of the People*, New York: Penguin, 1982.

Lieuwen, Edwin, *Generals vs. Presidents: Neo-militarism in Latin America*, New York: Praeger, 1964.

MacCameron, Robert, *Bananas, Labor and Politics in Honduras*, New York: Syracuse University Press, 1983.

MacLeod, Murdo J., *Spanish Central America: A Socioeconomic History 1520-1720*, Berkeley: University of California Press, 1973.

Mariñas Otero, Luis, *Honduras*, Madrid: Ediciones Cultura Hispánica, 1963.

Marshall, Jonathan, Peter Gale Scott and Jane Hunter, *The Iran-Contra Connection: Secret Teams and Covert Action in the Reagan Era*, Boston: South End Press, 1987.

Martínez Pelaez, Sucro, *La Patria del Criollo*, San José: EDUCA, 1979.

Mejía, Medardo, *Historia de Honduras*, Tegucigalpa: UNAH, 1983.

Meyer, Harry K., *Historical Dictionary of Honduras*, New York: Scarecrow, 1976.

Meza, Victor, *Historia del Movimiento Obrero Hondureño*, Tegucigalpa: Guaymuras, 1980.

Mills, C. Wright, *Power, Politics and People: The Views of C. Wright Mills*, London: Oxford, 1969.

Montúfar, Rafael, *Francisco Morazán*, San José: EDUCA, 1982.

Morris, James A., *Honduras: Caudillo Politics and Military Rulers*, Boulder and London: Westview, 1984.

———, "Honduras: An Oasis of Peace?" *Caribbean Review*, Vol. X, No. 1, Winter 1982.

Murga Frassinetti, Antonio, *Enclave y Sociedad en Honduras*, Tegucigalpa: Editorial Universitaria, 1978.

———, *La Crisis Económica en Honduras 1981-1984*, Tegucigalpa: CEDOH, 1984.

Nelson, Linda, *The Cost of Conquest: Indian Decline in Honduras Under Spanish Rule*, Boulder: Westview Press, 1976.

Neruda, Pablo, *Selected Poems*, New York: Grove Press, 1961.

Oqueli, Ramón, *La Víscera Entrañable*, Tegucigalpa: CEDOH, 1984.

Parker, Franklin, *The Central American Republics*, London: Royal Institute of International Affairs, 1971.

Pearce, Jenny, *Under the Eagle: U.S. Intervention in Central America and the Caribbean*, London: Latin America Bureau, 1982.

Peckenham, Nancy and Annie Street, *Honduras: Portrait of a Captive Nation*, New York: Praeger, 1985.

Persky, Stan, *The Last Domino: U.S. Foreign Policy in Central America Under Reagan*, Vancouver: New Star, 1984.

Posas, Mario y Rafael del Cid, *La Construcción del Sector Público y del Estado Nacional de Honduras 1976-1979*, San José: Ediciones Universitarias, 1981.

Posas, Mario, "Honduras at the Crossroads", *Latin American Perspectives*, No. 2 & 3, Spring and Summer 1980.

———, *El Movimiento Campesino Hondureño*, Tegucigalpa: Guaymuras, 1981.

Robicsek, Francis, *Copán: Home of the Mayan Gods*, New York: Museum of the American Indian Foundation, 1972.

Rodríguez, Mario, *A Palmerstonian Diplomat in Central America: Frederick Chatfield, Esq.*, Tucson: University of Arizona Press, 1964.

———, *Central America*, New Jersey: Prentice-Hall, 1965.

Ropp, Steve C., "The Honduran Army in the Sociopolitical Evolution of the Honduran State," *The Americas*, Vol. 30, No. 4, April 1974.

Rosenberg, Mark B., "Can Democracy Survive the Democrats?", unpublished article.

———, "Honduran Scorecard, Military and Democrats in Central America," *Caribbean Review*, Vol. XII No. 1, Winter 1983.

————, "Honduras: The Reluctant Democracy," *Current History*, Vol. 85, No. 515, December 1986.

————, "Nicaragua and Honduras: Toward Garrison States," *Current History*, Vol. 83, No. 490, February 1984.

Rosenberg, Mark and L. Shepherd, eds., *Honduras Confronts Its Future: Contending Perspectives and Critical Issues*, Boulder: Lynne Rienner, 1986.

Said, Edward W., *Covering Islam*, New York: Pantheon, 1981.

Selser, Gregorio, *Honduras, República Alquilada*, Mexico: Mex-sur, 1984.

Shaeffer, Louis, *O'Neill*, Boston: Little, Brown, 1968.

Sheehan, Edward R.F., "The Country of Nada," *New York Review of Books*, March 27, 1986.

Shepherd, Philip, "The Tragic Course and Consequence of U.S. Policy in Honduras", *World Policy Journal*, No. 1, Fall 1984.

Slutsky, Daniel y Esther Alonzo, *Empresas Transnacionales y Agricultura: el Caso del Enclave Bananero en Honduras*, Tegucigalpa: Ediciones Universitarias, 1980.

Soltera, María, *A Lady's Ride Across Honduras*, Gainsville: University of Florida, 1964.

Squier, E.G., *Honduras, A Historical and Statistical Description*, London: Tubner, 1870.

Stephens, J.L., *Incidents of Travel in Central America, Chiapas and Yucatan*, New York: Dover, 1841.

Stokes, S.W., *Honduras: An Area Study in Government*, Madison: University of Wisconsin, 1950.

Theroux, Paul, *The Mosquito Coast*, Boston: Houghton Mifflin, 1982.

The Tower Commission Report, New York: New York Times, 1987.

Valades, Eduardo, *Los Contratos del Diablo (las concesiones bananeros en Honduras)*, Mexico: Ediciónes Soc-Centro-Americanas, 1975.

Valle, Rafael Heliodoro, *Historia de la Cultura Hondureña*, Tegucigalpa: Ediciones Universitarias, 1981.

Volk, Stephen, "Honduras on the Border of War", *NACLA Report on the Americas*, Vol. xv, No. 6, Nov. / Dec., 1981.

Washington Office on Latin America, *Honduran Elections and Democracy: Withered by Washington*, Washington: WOLA, February 1986.

Wells, William V., *Explorations and Adventures in Honduras*, New York: Harper, 1857.

Wheaton, Philip, *Inside Honduras*, Washington: EPICA, 1982.

White, Richard Alan, *The Morass*, New York: Harper & Row, 1984.

Wilson, Charles Morrow, *Empire in Green and Gold*, New York: Holt, 1947.

Women's International Resource Exchange, *Honduran Women: The Marginalized Majority*, New York: WIRE, 1986.

Woodward, Ralph Lee Jr., *Central America: A Nation Divided*, New York: Oxford, 1976.

Zakus, Debra J., *Effecting Change: Education and the Lives of Rural Honduran Women,* unpublished M.A. thesis, 1984.

2. Periodicals

Boletín Informativo de Honduras, CEDOH, Tegucigalpa.
Central America Report, Toronto.
Honduras Update, Boston.
Latin America Weekly Report, London.
Mesoamérica, San José, Costa Rica.
NACLA Report on the Americas, New York.
Honduras Briefing, London.
and various union and political periodicals from Honduras.

Appendix I: The Face of Underdevelopment

Infant mortality – 78 per thousand.

Life expectancy – 62.*

Access to social security – 10% of total population: 13% of workers.

Daily calorie consumption – 1,800 (83% of requirement).

Children under 5 suffering from some degree of malnutrition – 72.5%.

Illiteracy rate – 40.4%, 84% in the countryside.

Birth rate – more than 3%.

Housing needs – 450,000.

Housing constructed between 1970 and 1984 – 51,916.

Housing needs of rural population – 78%.

Housing built for rural population – 8%.

Source: Honduran Secretary of Economic Planning, March 1987.

* Please note that the CIA World Fact Book, as cited in chapter one, gives life expectancy as 58 years.

Appendix II: U.S. Aid to Central America 1980-87

					(millions $)			
	1980	1981	1982	1983	1984	1985	1986	1987
HONDURAS								
military	4.0	8.9	31.3	37.3	77.5	62.5	88.2	81.5
economic	51.0	33.9	78.0	101.2	209.0	138.9	157.9	156.1
Total	55.0	42.8	109.3	138.5	286.5	201.4	246.1	238.2
EL SALVADOR								
military	6.0	35.5	82.0	81.3	196.5	128.2	132.6	132.6
economic	57.8	133.6	182.2	231.1	331.1	326.1	350.8	319.3
Total	63.8	169.1	264.2	312.4	527.6	454.3	483.4	441.9
GUATEMALA								
military	0.0	0.0	0.0	0.0	0.0	0.3	10.3	5.6
economic	11.1	16.6	23.9	17.6	33.3	73.8	77.2	139.0
Total	11.1	16.6	23.9	17.6	33.3	74.1	87.5	144.6
COSTA RICA								
military	0.0	0.3	2.1	2.6	9.2	9.2	2.7	2.4
economic	14.0	13.3	120.6	212.4	177.9	208.0	187.3	118.1
Total	14.0	13.6	122.7	215.0	187.1	217.2	190.0	120.5

Source: U.S. Agency for International Development

Index

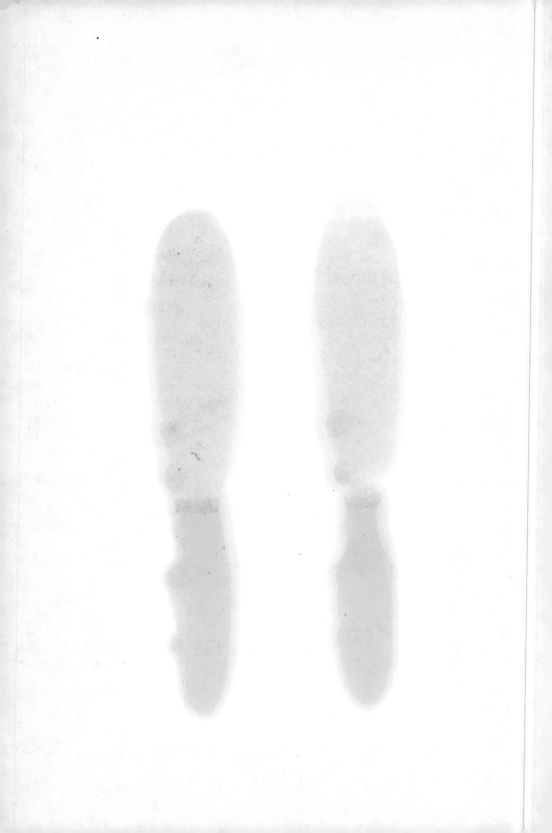